# THE WAY WE CARE

*By the same Author:*

# THE WAY WE CARE

by Gilbert Kirby

SCRIPTURE UNION
5 Wigmore Street, London WIH OAD

First published 1973

ISBN 0 85421 407 0



Photoset and printed in Malta by St Paul's Press Ltd.

## CONTENTS

## FOREWORD

This small book makes no pretensions to being a "magnum opus" in the realm of Christian ethics. Much of it basically represents lecture material given to students of London Bible College. The inevitable price of touching on a fairly wide variety of topics is that none of them can be dealt with at great length, and inevitably some topics have had to be discussed at a more superficial level than others.

Truly Biblical Christianity has always shown a concern for the whole man, although some Christians have been accused of putting their exclusive emphasis on "pie in the sky". Happily there is today a healthy revival of interest in the social implications of the gospel on the part of those Christians who, while having an overriding concern for man's spiritual welfare, also recognize that God is concerned for body, soul and spirit. These Christians are in the tradition of such evangelical stalwarts as William Wilberforce, the Earl of Shaftesbury, Thomas Barnardo and William Booth. It is an encouraging sign that in recent years the subject of Christian ethics has been increasingly in demand in our theological colleges. Younger as well as older Christians are keenly aware of ethical issues.

A book such as this may quickly date, since, with the rapid advancement of medical science and technology, problems constantly arise which have ethical implications. We have tried to foresee one or two of these issues. We are bound to add that with every passing year the application of Christian ethical ideals to our increasingly complex society becomes more difficult. We nevertheless concur with the view that "the Church should speak a discerning word to each concrete situation."

On many of the issues raised the debate will continue for a long time to come. Some of the conclusions reached here may well prove to be interim ones, and on some issues varying viewpoints have been expressed without definite conclusions being reached. When we speak of Christian principles, such as are clearly delineated in Scripture, we can speak with the utmost authority, but when it comes to the application of those principles to some of the more complex problems of our modern society, there must be room for manoeuvre. This book will have served its purpose if it succeeds in stimulating its readers to undertake a more detailed and thoughtful study of the Scriptures themselves and is also the means of convincing them that being a Christian affects a man's whole life—his attitude to his home and family, to his neighbours, to the community as a whole.

We have taken the liberty of quoting freely from a number of contemporary works, and the serious student of the subject will, no doubt, wish to delve more deeply into many of these books. It is a cause for shame that until recently all too few books on the subject of Christian ethics have been written by those who would be happily identified as evangelical Christians. We are thankful to know that the position is being rectified—this volume represents a very modest contribution to that end.

Among the topics to which all too little attention has been given is that of violence and revolution. Moreover, a great deal more thinking needs to be done by Christian people about applying Christian principles to modern industry, and also in the field of medicine.

Whatever imperfections the book has, it might have had more were it not for the helpful advice received from Mr. Michael Hews, Book Editor of the Scripture Union, and other good friends. A special word of gratitude is due to my Secretary, Miss Brenda Donaldson, who typed almost all of the manuscripts, and in a variety of ways eased my burdens so that the writing of such a book became a practical possibility.

# 1. AN INTRODUCTION TO ETHICS

Ethics is the science which enquires into the meaning and purpose of life and of conduct. It represents a systematic attempt to consider the purposeful actions of mankind, to determine their rightness or wrongness, their tendency to good or evil. When a man asks "What ought I to do about it?" he is raising an ethical problem. The questioner assumes that there is a right and a wrong mode of action. Conduct, as that word is used in ethics, may be defined as conscious and purposeful action, or action directed to an end.

Any religion worthy of consideration has ethical content and implications, while irreligion and atheism are essentially non-ethical. Karl Marx declared in the Communist Manifesto—"Law, morality, religion are... so many bourgeois prejudices, behind which lurk in ambush just as many bourgeois interests." When God is banished from human thought, ethics and morality either become non-existent or wholly relative and dictated largely by expediency. Thus actions are weighed as to whether they are appropriate or inappropriate to the system.

Ethics could be described as the science of moral duty, designed to determine ideal human character and the ideal end of human action. Ethics relates to inner motivation as well as to the outward manner of life.

The question we are bound to ask is—"Where is the foundation for morality in the world today?" With the present widespread rejection of all forms of belief in the supernatural, there has come an increasing revolt against the specifically Christian ethics which asks, "Since God has so acted, what ought we to do?"

The study of the various ethical systems which have been put forward, each claiming to be the right one, is termed "general ethics". While the student of general ethics must debate the relative merits and defects of the various systems he encounters, the student of Christian ethics starts with the assumption that that which God commands is right and that in the Bible is the revelation of God's will for men.

Morality, the conforming of men to virtuous principles of conduct, is not, of course, the exclusive property of the Christian Church. Natural ethics could be described as a result of human thought and reflection over the centuries in man's search for the "good life". The Christian does not deny that there are elements of truth in natural ethics, but he claims that in Christ he has a new and higher standard as well as a new motive for the pursuit of that standard, and a new power to enable him to attain it. The conception of human nature held by Christians, who regard man as a spiritual being, created in the image of God, and destined to immortality, is very different from the conception held by those for whom man is simply a product of evolution with no life other than that on this planet.

The man who has rejected the Christian religion will not find it easy to accept Christian ethics since Christian ethics depend on Christian theology. Christians, however, maintain that the Christian moral law is not just a private code of conduct for Christians, but the revelation of God's will for all men at all times and at all stages of their development.

There are various ways in which the aim of right conduct may be conceived such as, for example, the attainment of some "supreme good" or "summum bonum". This "supreme good" will be, for the Moslem, the enjoyment of the pleasures of Paradise; for the Christian, union with Christ; for the Hindu, delivery from the burden of individual existence and re-absorption into Brahma; for the Buddhist, freedom from the burden of all existence and extinction in Nirvana.

For others the ethical ideal relates to the formation of a particular character. Here the goal is seen in man rather than outside him; as something he must strive to be, rather than something he desires to possess. For Plato the ideal character was the wise man, or philosopher; for Aristotle, the ideal was the "magnificent" man; for the Christian the ideal is the "man of God".

Another ethical concept points to a law which must be obeyed by all who seek perfection—an objective moral code which is to be regarded as binding. Yet others have seen as their ethical ideal the gaining or avoiding of certain feelings or emotions. Here the emphasis is on such emotions as pleasure; tranquillity, or satisfaction, rather than anything permanent, such as character.

The promotion of certain social conditions is the objective of yet other ethical idealists. The aim might be described, for example, as being "the greatest good of the greatest number". The emphasis is upon social responsibility so that the ethical ideal is seen more and more to transcend the merely personal.

Sooner or later men reach a stage when they ask not merely what is allowed or forbidden, but why? In other words, "What are our presuppositions?"

In the case of Christians, ethical presuppositions have a theological basis. The question of right and wrong is related to that which is commanded or forbidden by God.

Thus the moral law is the expression of God's will. Christian ethics assume the fact of God and the fact that He has made His will known.

For the Epicurean, on the other hand, virtue is identified as that conduct which, on the whole and in the long-run, yields most happiness and least pain; while vice is that which, in the long-run and on the whole, yields most pain and least pleasure. Thus gluttony and drunkenness are wrong simply because in the long-run they yield more pain than pleasure. Conversely, kindness, unselfishness, and suchlike qualities, are to be sought because in the long-run they bring their own reward.

The Stoics held that virtue was to be sought for its own sake quite apart from its results. It was believed that there was a natural law which man could know and could obey, and conformity to this law was the highest good. Man could know what was right and wrong intuitively. The individual must find the "mind of nature" and cultivate an impassive disposition. "Apathy" became the key word of Stoic ethics.

Those with purely utilitarian presuppositions do not ask the question "Is it good?" but "Is it useful?"—"What is its utility value?" Lying, murder and theft are wrong not primarily because they do not promote the greatest good of the greatest number, but because they are, if generally indulged in, incompatible with the existence of civilised society.

Today we hear much of the so-called ethic of relativism: what may be esteemed a proper moral standard in a given culture is, by the premises of this ethic, not necessarily a universal principle. For some, social ethics have almost entirely replaced personal ethics, and if a man holds enlightened views about society as a whole, he is considered moral. The so-called "ethic of the aesthetic" declares that the natural thing is the proper and right thing to do, while the existentialist ethic is content to make out a case for one's duty to humanity in the face of a completely meaningless universe. The existentialist denies that we have any genuinely objective clues to right conduct. "Any end chosen", comments Sartre, "has value only because it is chosen."

In all these ethical systems there may well be an element of truth, but none of itself is wholly satisfactory. It has been said that the extent to which we succeed in giving a full, true and exhaustive answer to the question, "What is man?" will be the extent to which we are in a position to draw out a coherent system of general laws relating to human conduct. While, as we shall see later, the Bible does not minimise the wickedness of the human heart, neither does it overlook the essential dignity of man who was "made a little lower than the angels." Man is no mere cog in a machine with no special significance, but a creature of infinite worth, someone, in fact, for whom the very Son of God was even prepared to die. Furthermore, the Bible assumes a life beyond the grave and truly Christian ethics have to be evaluated against the backcloth, not only of time, but of eternity.

## 2. SITUATION ETHICS AND THE NEW MORALITY

A morality based on God's commands can only be relevant to those who believe in God. In an age such as this a morality with a supernatural foundation is limited in its appeal.

The so-called "new moralists" claim to deal realistically with our predicament. They begin with two basic assumptions. First, "that all men do, whether Christians or not, as a matter of psychological fact experience the transcendent claim of love in some personal relationship; and, second, that provided men understand the facts of the situation they need only ask themselves what would love do in it and the correct answer will occur to them". Joseph Fletcher in his book, *Situation Ethics*, spells out this philosophy: "Christian situation ethics has only one norm or principle or law, call it what you will, that is binding and unexceptionable, always good and right regardless of the circumstances—that is 'love'." There is no such thing as a predefinition of goodness or badness.

The "new morality" says that no line of action may be prescribed before the event, and what is wrong in one set of circumstances and personal relationships may in another situation be a response to the claim of love. This could even apply to sexual relations outside marriage. This ethical theory claims to meet the needs of a generation that spurns all external authority (the State, the Church, the Bible, parents), yet still seeks for a directive. The "ethics of a situation", we are told, is to be determined by the content of the situation. Ethics are thus not absolute but "existential" or "situational".

In his book *Christian Morals Today*, Dr. J. A. T. Robinson complains that the phrase "the new morality" is "bandied about in the wildest manner". He points out that he was not responsible for coining the phrase, nor had it in origin anything to do with sex, but rather with existentialism, or "situation ethics". A book entitled *The New Morality*, by G. E. Newson was, in fact, published as long ago as 1932.

The new moralists reject the category of law, and claim biblical warrant for so doing. They refer to Paul's teaching regarding the ineffectiveness of the Law to secure either man's justification or sanctification (Romans 8:3,4). We need to recognise, however, that the apostle does *not* repudiate the Law as the standard of conduct. He sees the observance of the Law as the *result* of justification, and as being of the essence of sanctification although not its means.

John Robinson is anxious to see Christian ethics shake itself loose from the supports of "super-naturalistic legalism". What is needed in place of the traditional morality, he says, is "a radical ethic of the situation with nothing prescribed except love". "Nothing", he boldly reiterates, "can of itself always be labelled as wrong".

In the book *Christian Morals Today*, Robinson explains his views. "The old morality," he states, "locates the unchanging element in Christian ethics in the content of the commands. There are certain things which are always right, and others which are always wrong. These absolute Christian standards are eternally valid, and remain unchanging in the midst of relativity and flux.

And it is this body of moral teaching, grounded firmly on the laws of God and the commands of Christ, which the Church exists to proclaim to every succeeding generation of men and women, whether they hear or whether they forbear." The new morality, by contrast, denies that there is an ethical code of abiding validity: the only thing that remains unchanging is the unconditional claim of God upon man. Traditional morality, Robinson argues, must be jettisoned. It is not acceptable to the modern generation. "In Christian ethics the only pure statement is the command to love: every other injunction depends on it and is an explication or application of it." "Love is the end, the 'telos' of the law, not merely in the sense that it fulfils it (which it does), but in the sense that it abolishes it as the foundation of the Christian's responsibility, whether with God or man". "We cannot," he says, "pretend to have the answers in advance". In certain situations even an act of treachery may be an act of love, according to John Robinson.

The new moralists erect an inflexible principle of their own—love for them is the one great absolute. "Whatever is the most loving thing in the situation is the right and good thing." They argue that our Lord in His debate with the Pharisees championed love against law.

In his Reith Lectures, Professor C. M. Carstairs stated, "In our religious traditions the essence of morality has sometimes appeared to consist of sexual restraint. But this was not emphasised in Christ's own teaching. For Him the cardinal virtue was charity, that is, consideration of and concern for other people." The Dean of Trinity College, Cambridge, the Rev. H. A. Williams, in a contribution to the symposium *Soundings*, makes a similar point and calls for "A re-assessment of moral values." The report, *Towards a Quaker View of Sex*, called in question the validity of traditional sexual morality, while Robinson in *Honest to God* pointed out that traditional morality is oppressively legalistic: "The moral precepts of Jesus are not intended to be understood legalistically as prescribing what all Christians must do, whatever the circumstances, and pronouncing certain courses of action universally right and others universally wrong." Fletcher argues it is better to live together unmarried in commitment and loyalty and responsibility than to live in marriage with no love.

Undoubtedly many of the new moralists are seriously and sincerely endeavouring to grapple with moral issues, but there are certain basic defects in their reasoning.

They begin by assuming that men in general feel the undisputed claim of love upon them. But is it not a disastrous mistake to think that love of itself is the absolute norm for human conduct? The absolute norm is God's will, albeit expressed in love. Once grant that, and we are bound to ask, can the will of God be read off from a set of human circumstances without reference to some prior revelation of that divine will? As Henlee Barnette says in *The New Theology and Morality*, "If love is not defined in terms of objective ethical guide-lines, such as chastity, charity and concern for others, and grounded in the living Christ, it has no adequate dynamic and dissolves into sentimentality."

The advocates of situation ethics show an unbounded, almost naive, confidence in human ability, and overlook human sinfulness. Man's fallen nature makes him adept at evasion, rationalisation and self-excuse. Situational ethics ignores man's fallen nature. What he is conditions what he will do. A truly biblical ethic sees man as he is, created in God's image and yet in a fallen condition. If a man is a sinner and if Christian ethics are the ethics of the redeemed, then reconciliation is required as a prime requisite. Christian ethics diverge most sharply from every type of secular ethics in the basic presupposition that a man must be "born again". The formula

"I ought but I cannot" summarises the predicament of fallen and unregenerate man. It is only the man who is spiritually reborn who can heed the call to imitate Christ. The New Testament presents as a fundamental fact in the moral life the presence and power of the indwelling Holy Spirit. While in part the new morality is a reaction against legalism it also represents man's recurrent temptation to over-estimate himself, his reason and his essential goodness.

In the final analysis the new morality is man-centred rather than God-centred. Love is defined in terms of concern for the other man, not in terms of obedience to the commands of God.

Furthermore, as William Barclay points out, "situation ethics presents us with a terrifying degree of freedom." There is nowhere for man to turn for clear-cut guidance as to what he should do. It is highly questionable whether man is ready or ever likely to be ready for such freedom. We could not begin to contemplate a football match devoid of both referee and rules. On the road we have our highway code. Is it not equally necessary in the light of our fallen human nature that we should be given objective instructions for the journey of life? The fact that we recognise the place of law need not make us legalistic. Freedom and law must go hand in hand. It is by the influence of the law that men and women come in the end to be truly free.

## 3. OLD TESTAMENT BACKGROUND

The ethics of the New Testament is firmly grounded in the revelation given in the Old Testament, so let us look first at the Old Testament. The distinctive character of Hebrew ethics is that it is theological ethics. The basic biblical presupposition is that there is a personal God, and that the God revealed in the Scriptures is the one true God. Old Testament ethics is founded upon the being and character of God—upon the reality of an absolute and objective moral order which proceeds from and is the expression of the will of a holy God.

God to the Hebrew mind was not an abstraction. He was the "living God" whose nature and power were being constantly manifested in the lives of men. The God of the Bible is the One who stands behind nature and controls it, and who may use it to reveal something of His glory. His activity could be expressed alike through natural events or through events contrary to the course of nature. This God played a special part in Israel's history, having chosen her for Himself and declared His will to her. To Israel God was personal and His personality expressed itself in moral requirements. God revealed His character in His activity, and there was a moral purpose governing it. Thus the religion of Israel is ethical in its essence and not merely in its demands.

The God whom Israel worshipped was to them the source and sanction of the moral law which He progressively revealed to them. Morality then was the embodied will of God.

God's essential sovereignity makes His law for men inseparable from His glory. The glory of God is frequently mentioned in the Old Testament—He is conceived of as one before whom men are constrained to bow in reverence and adoration. Every departure from the revealed law of God is an affront to the glory of God. The right to command resides in the majesty of His person and is expressed in the absoluteness of His will. His sovereignty derives from the Creator/creature relationship, and since man was made in the moral image of God moral obedience is required from him. Moral law is the expression in human life of unchangeable moral principles proceeding from God.

It was the common belief of the Puritans that when the Creator formed man He gave him "a law of universal obedience written in his heart which by his fall was much obliterated and defaced: yet all mankind have some fragments of it remaining in their hearts; such as make the very Gentiles who have not the written law inexcusable for their transgressions".

In the Old Testament the Hebrew word *qodesh* (holiness) and its derivatives occur more than 830 times. The word suggests both withdrawal and consecration—withdrawal from that which is unclean, and consecration to that which is sacred and pure. Applied to God it signifies His separation from and transcendency over all creation; His supremacy, majesty and awesome glory, as well as the ethical spotlessness of His character.

The biblical concept of holiness properly understood stands for all in God's being that cannot be grasped by mere reason, all that towers up in infinite sublimity over man and the world. The ethical is linked with the numinous—the response to the revelation of God's mysterious holiness is a deep sense of one's own sinfulness (cf. Isaiah 6:5). Holiness, signifying the essential nature of

God, includes in it the notion of righteousness—it is the most comprehensive name for the divine moral perfection. God the perfect being is the epitome of holiness, and men are holy in proportion as their lives are godlike.

In the Old Testament human morality is based on divine morality. The holiness of God is a challenge to men to imitate it (Leviticus 19:2). Brunner points out that the special characteristic of Christian ethics is that it is "the science of human conduct as it is determined by divine conduct". The Hebrew idea of perfection was not derived from an analysis of the characters of noble men, but from the essential moral character of God.

Among ethical teachers we find conflicting theories regarding human nature. One view is that man by nature is morally good—his natural impulses are from birth wholly virtuous, and require only to be left to their own operation to issue in a life of perfection. Among the Greeks, especially the Stoics, this view prevailed. Such a view, however, is in harmony neither with Scripture nor experience, and underlying biblical ethics is the fact of human sin—the fallenness of man. Various terms for sin are used in the Bible, but common to them all is the idea of disharmony with the will of God. The fundamental character of sin is that it comes between a man and God, and isolates him from his Maker (Genesis 3:8). All sin is against God. Salvation, therefore, must essentially be God's act in restoring the relationship between man and God which is broken by sin. No system of ethics can claim to be Christian which ignores the fact that human nature is in some way corrupted. Man is morally responsible and accountable to God. When he violates the known will of God he thereby incurs the divine wrath. The Old Testament reveals retributive justice as an essential principle of the moral order. As sin is disobedience, so the essence of morality is loving obedience to the known will of God.

Old Testament ethics is founded upon a covenant relationship between God and His people. God's covenant love (*chesed*) is shown in mercy and grace, which in turn call forth the response of dutiful obedience from man. The idea of the covenant is fundamental to both the Old and New Testaments. The covenant which God made with His people at Sinai was frequently recalled and renewed throughout Old Testament history, and served as a type of the new covenant predicted by Jeremiah (Jeremiah 31:31), and fulfilled in the New Testament. It was a covenant initiated by God as an act of His grace.

The Law as given through Moses set forth the conditions on which God would continue to dwell in covenant relationship with His people. The giving of the Law was seen to be an act of favour on God's part, and a great honour to the nation. Law follows upon covenant as its outward sign. The Ten Commandments epitomize the basic demands of Israel's faith.

The Law was the embodiment of the divine will. In it are set forth man's duties to God and his neighbour. T. W. Manson points out that the Torah differs in three important respects from what we usually call law. The scope is wider—it deals with the whole life of the Israelite; for example, it even touches on the thought life: "Thou shalt not covet." The manner of its promulgation is different—it is oracular rather than statutory, and is transmitted authoritatively through priests or prophets. Its provisions are irreformable and incapable of repeal.

All this follows from the fact that the Law was nothing less than the revealed will of God as Israel's King. As Paul demonstrates, the Law was in fact a vehicle of God's redemptive purposes also, since it pointed beyond itself (Galatians 3:24).

The comprehensiveness of the Decalogue as a sum-mary of moral obligation is demonstrated by the fact that under the full light of New Testament moral teaching, it has continued to be used for catechetical purposes by nearly every church in the world. D. Elton Trueblood in his book *Foundations for Reconstruction* asserts that "The Ten Commandments constitute the most memorable and succinct extant formulation of the ethical creed of the West..." They provide a convenient statement of the fundamental basis of recovery and reconstruction "in a world wherein the problem of moral reconstruction is the primary problem." He stresses the importance of "the total view of life of which the classic commandments are shorthand presentations. Each of the commandments can be greatly expanded; each can be stated in positive rather than negative form... When this is done, we have...positive principles of such a nature that a good society cannot be constructed or reconstructed without reference to them."

The eighth-century prophets recalled men to obedience to the basic principles of Israel's religion. Ethical monotheism found its highest expression in their utterances. Men such as Isaiah, Amos and Micah fulminated against social injustice. They attacked formal religion and called for justice and impartiality. They were preachers of personal righteousness. They were also apostles of hope, often uttering greater things than they themselves knew.

Consistently the Old Testament insists that there can be no religion without ethics. The service of God and the service of men must go always hand in hand (cf. Micah 6:6–8). The prophets did not mince their words. Their pronouncements covered many practical details of everyday life. We heartily concur in the judgment of William Barclay: "There are few more wonderful ethics than the ethic of the Old Testament. It has its sternness and it has its severity, but it has its mercy and its kindness and its love. It is the very basis of the Christian ethic, and the Christian ethic could not have had a greater base or a finer cradle."

## 4. OUR LORD'S ETHICAL TEACHING

It is important to remember that Christ's moral teaching presupposes that of the Old Testament. This helps to explain why He said so little concerning social righteousness. God's mind concerning that had been revealed already through the prophets. He taught little concerning the family: the law-books of the Pentateuch had long since given the divine ruling on these matters. Christ did not abrogate the moral principles of the Old Testament: He came "not to destroy but to fulfil".

It is even difficult to show that there was anything startlingly "new" in Christ's moral precepts. To a considerable extent they could all be paralleled from the Old Testament or the writings of Confucius, the Buddha, Plato or the Stoics. What, however, is original and unparalleled is that Jesus made Himself the centre of His teaching. He did not merely teach truth: He claimed to be its living embodiment. His teaching cannot be understood in isolation from His Person and His Mission. He was not primarily a Teacher but a Saviour. His message was not primarily the setting forth of a new morality but the proclamation of good news. The *didache* (teaching) must be studied in the context of the *kerygma*—the proclamation of what God had done through Him: His perfect life, His death, His resurrection and exaltation to be a Prince and Saviour. However, although Christ was not primarily a moral Teacher He is foremost among them. Here, as everywhere, He is preeminent.

Jesus (like Socrates) wrote nothing. His ethical remarks, it has been said, are so many *obiter dicta*—as perplexing and paradoxical and contrary to ordinary human standards as His actions and character (W. F. Lofthouse). His teaching cannot be systematised.

Christ was not a speculative thinker, a philosopher dealing in abstractions. He dealt with men and women in concrete situations. Nor was He a detached and unpractical visionary but a man amongst men: like the Old Testament prophets, a man of action, intimately in touch with the life of His time.

Christ lifted morality out of legalism and based it on love. He did not point to a law to be obeyed as an external rule of righteousness: "for righteousness' sake" He equated with "for my sake" (Matt. 5:10,11). He summoned disciples with the call, "Follow Me." His teaching was authoritarian and absolute, not relative and subjective. "He taught as one who had authority". Christ's teaching is categorical. He issued commandments, moral imperatives, which, though they constitute a "law" are not mere legal enactments. They are moral principles; but His precept of love was more than an exhortation: it was a "new commandment". His is an ethic of law and duty (Cf. the law of Christ, Gal. 6:2; the perfect law of liberty, James 1:25). It was the ultimate fulfilment of the law of Moses.

Christ's law is independent of time and place and, also, of consequences. To adapt Kant's words, the Christian is expected to be able to say, "I will obey Christ though the heavens fall!"

Even some non-Christian philosophers, such as Plato, recognised that moral law must be objective, eternal, unchangeable, transcendent and not relative to time, place, custom, desire, convenience, prudence, etc. The problem was to say what was the source, the ground and the goal of morality. (Cf. Plato's "Form of the Good" or Kant's "Law of Universality"). The Christian believes, with the Old Testament prophets, that the moral law is the law of God, a transcript of His character. Morality, then, is not primarily human self-seeking, self-realisation, self-fulfilment (though these motives are all appealed to) but consists essentially in doing the will of God. Christ's teaching is neither hedonistic nor merely prudential. Its promise of human blessedness and self-realisation is bound up with man's conformity to the will and character of God. He says (John 7:17) "If any man will do his will, he shall know of the doctrine whether it be of God". The emphasis is on the will rather than the intellect; nevertheless obedience of will leads to knowledge of truth. And Christ is the Truth. To know Christ means more than mere intellectual apprehension: it involves committal of the will, moral committal.

Another point to bear in mind about Christ's ethical teaching is that it is not nationalistic but universal in its scope. "Thy neighbour" to the Israelite meant a fellow-Hebrew; to Christ it meant anyone—even an hereditary enemy like the hated Samaritan. "Many shall come from the east and the west...", said our Lord.

We may well ask—"Who is sufficient for these things?" The answer is that Christ's ethic is not a humanistic but a supernatural ethic. The Christian ethic is made possible only through the promise of the Holy Spirit. It presupposes regeneration ("You must be born anew"—words which were a fulfilment of the prophecies of Jer. 31:31 ff. and Ezek. 36:26–27) and divine grace (John 15:5– "apart from Me you can do nothing").

Some of Christ's precepts do raise problems of exegesis. How are we to understand some of the perplexing sayings of Jesus: for example, "Sell what you possess and give it to the poor"; "Do not lay up for yourselves treasure on earth"; "Love your enemies"; "If your right eye causes you to sin, pluck it out"; "Give to him who begs from you"? Are they to be taken literally? Should we say that they were meant to be taken literally but are impracticable? Or should we say they are not to be understood in a literal sense, but are graphic expressions of an ideal type of human nature? And, might it not be also true that they represent impossible demands deliberately made to show the need for supernatural grace?

Osborn in *Christian Ethics* emphasises that the sayings of Jesus are not to be understood as legal enactments designed to regulate every conceivable situation, but as concrete embodiments of fundamental principles.

Christ's method was to bring specific cases under general principles. The most fundamental ethical principle was primarily religious and secondarily social, it was a personal attitude, namely, love to God and love to one's neighbour. The first was to be absolute: "with all your heart, and with all your soul, and with all your mind"; the second was to be relative to oneself "and... your neighbour as yourself". (See Matt. 22:35–40 and cf. Luke 10:25–37). This latter is the so-called "Golden Rule" (Matt. 7:12 cf. Rom. 13:8–10, Gal. 5:14). James calls this the "royal law, according to the Scripture" (ch. 2 v 8).

A further important principle of interpretation is to recognise that the moral injunctions of our Lord are not all in the same category. Anderson Scott classifies them as *mandata, exempla* and *consilia*.

By *mandata* he means commandments proper. Of these he finds only one: "You shall love..." (Mark 12:30,31; Luke 10:25–27). L. H. Marshall in *The Challenge of New Testament Ethics* extends this category to include "those imperatives which state principles which all who are in the Kingdom have accepted". Among these he includes general attitudes such as love to God and one's neighbour, the "Golden Rule" and the command to repent; and such specific *mandata* as the prohibition of swearing and retaliation; love to one's enemies; teaching concerning mammon (Matt. 6:19ff, Luke 12:33f) and the need for seeking first God's Kingdom (Matt. 6:33).

*Exempla* is used of illustrations of particular ways in which principles can be applied. Thus, in Matt. 5:38–42 after condemning the spirit of vindictiveness, Christ gives four "lightning sketches of a non-vindictive spirit in actual operation" in the four sayings about turning the other cheek, giving the cloak as well as the tunic, going the second mile and giving to one that asks for help. These sayings are not rules for all occasions but concrete examples of the kind of behaviour Christ has in mind, "He means them quite literally and thinks of them as being literally followed" says L. H. Marshall in *The Challenge of New Testament Ethics* (p. 125). Anderson Scott, however, affirms: "There is no obligation upon Christians to understand them or to act upon them literally." The individual Christian must give some thought to this and make up his own mind.

*Concilia* are sayings giving "urgent advice", spoken to particular persons and in particular circumstances. Perhaps the best example is the statement to the rich young ruler, "If you would be perfect, go, sell what you possess. . ." (Matt. 19:21). In those very early Christian writings, the *Didache* and the *Shepherd of Hermas*, a distinction was drawn between "Counsels" and "Precepts". This distinction in time led to a false categorization of works which were supererogatory and those that were obligatory. In the mediaeval church a differentiation was made between "commandments" and "judgments", between that which is necessary and that which is advisable, between precepts of obedience and counsels of perfection. Those who aspired to be obedient to the "consilia" were regarded as building up for themselves special merit—a doctrine which finds no place in the New Testament.

If there is one word more than another which sums up the teaching and attitude of Christ it is "concern". He taught that God Himself cares infinitely for men and women and they in turn must be concerned for their fellows. What is more, our concern for one another must be total—body, soul and spirit. Evangelical Christians sometimes speak of "a passion for souls", but we should be concerned for the whole man. The Christian ethic, as Jesus Christ Himself enunciated it, may be summed up in the one Greek word, *agape*. This is no sentimental word, nor does it have romantic associations, rather it implies concern for the good of men and women in the fullest possible sense and to the highest degree. Such concern found its fullest expression on the Cross when the sinless Son of God Himself died the most shameful death, "the just for the unjust that He might bring us to God."

## 5. OBJECTIONS TO CHRIST'S ETHICAL TEACHING

Christ has often been accused of Utopianism and has been represented as a visionary, whose ethics are on a plane too exalted for man to attain. It is clear, however, that He intended His teaching should be practised (Matt. 28:19–20).

G. K. Chesterton once remarked "The Sermon on the Mount has not been tried and found wanting; it has been found difficult and not tried." The natural man looks for a more moderate ethic, based on prudence and expediency, rather than the high idealism set by Christ.

Sometimes Christ's teaching has been misunderstood and even rejected because of a failure to recognise that He makes abundant use of oriental imagery. Only absurd literalness would lead anyone to suppose, for example, that hatred of kith and kin is a precondition of Christian discipleship. Many of the criticisms directed against our Lord's teaching are based upon a misunderstanding of what He actually meant, and a failure to recognise that Jesus was concerned, not so much with rules and regulations, but with an attitude of mind and heart. It is folly to interpret His words as if they were simply clauses in a code of law. Christ often spoke in such a way as to startle men from their complacency and compel them to heed His teaching.

Just because the ideal that was set for us by our Lord is high, it should not be dismissed as impracticable. What would be the use to mankind of an ideal easily attainable? In any case, our Lord's teaching is sometimes more practicable, and practical, than appears on the surface. The natural man, for example, argues strongly in favour of retaliation. We all know from experience in ordinary everyday life that to meet insult and wrong with wrong is often to make matters worse and add fuel to the fire. The methods advocated by our Lord may be difficult, but they prove, in fact, to be more realistic and practical than those advocated by worldly men.

The non-Christian tends to overlook the fact that the ethics of Jesus are religious ethics, the ethics of the Kingdom of God. It is only when seen in this light that they become intelligible and practicable. The ideals of Jesus are for men who are in touch with the power of God and who know the Kingdom of God within them.

Critics of Christianity claim that it is impossible for anyone to be a real Christian unless he turns his back upon the world, its interests, its possessions, its pleasures, and gives himself up solely to the private quest of holiness of life. It is true, of course, that at various times in the history of the Christian Church there have been those that have opted for celibacy, the renunciation of property and wealth, and the monastic life. Both the Roman Catholic and the Greek Orthodox Churches have introduced a double standard of ethics—the higher, for those who renounce the world and choose the monastic life, and the lower for those who remain in the world. Borrowing University terminology, one may say that monks and nuns gain ethical honours, while other Christians settle for an ethical pass degree! There have always been those who have found elements in the teaching of our Lord which appear not only to justify, but to require the ascetic life, as, for example, our Lord's words to the rich, young ruler. The famous "eunuch" passage (Matt. 19:12) has caused some Christians to regard celibacy as the ideal. They forget that, taking our Lord's teaching as a whole, it is clear that He regarded marriage as natural and normal in the lives of most men and women, while at the same time pointing out that there will be those who are ready voluntarily to renounce marriage for the sake of the Kingdom of God.

It is clear that our Lord Himself was far from being an ascetic. Had He been ascetically inclined He would surely have shown some affinity with the Jewish monastic order, the Essenes. In fact He entered so freely into social life that He was denounced as "a glutton and a drunkard" (Matt. 11:19). He had no antipathy to material things as such. It is significant that the twelve apostles did not become ascetics. Almost all the virtues which our Lord extols are virtues which can be exercised only in ordinary social relationships. A man can hardly act as a "good Samaritan" if he spends all his time in a monastic cell! Our Lord's ethical teaching is clearly geared to men and women who live in the world. In His high-priestly prayer—"I do not pray that thou shouldest take them out of the world, but that Thou shouldest keep them from the evil one" (Jn. 17:15).

As Dr. Hensley Henson has pointed out, the criticism that Christianity is ascetic "fails to distinguish between the asceticism of self-discipline and the asceticism of self-mutilation, between that which aims at bringing the body under control, and that which aspires to belittle, suppress and, in a sense, annihilate the body. The one vindicates, the other destroys, the right balance of human nature... Christianity is unquestionably ascetic in the one sense and as unquestionably non-ascetic in the other." Self-discipline is indeed inseparable from Christian discipleship. It is for the Christian to seek to be morally and spiritually fit, as the athlete seeks to be physically fit, and neither type of fitness can be attained without a measure of self-sacrifice. Because a Christian aims at holiness of life, he holds lightly to ephemeral pleasures and bodily delights. He must be no great lover of comfort or of luxury, for these things are apt to be debilitating to the soul.

Christ's teaching has also been criticised on the grounds that it is excessively benevolent. It has been pointed out that the saying "Give to him who begs from you", if taken literally might, in fact, harm the beggar himself and will encourage begging and possibly cause a man to rob himself and his family of their dues, in order to make provision for a parasitical member of society. In meeting this criticism one must again point out that a narrow, literal interpretation of our Lord's sayings gives a gross misrepresentation of His meaning. Our Lord did not *always* heal the sick. Sometimes He turned from the needy crowds and sought rest for Himself and His disciples (Mk. 6:31–32). What was good had to be sacrificed for what would be far better on the whole and in the long run. His basic emphasis was that we should love our neighbours *as* ourselves, and this implies a due and proper regard for oneself.

Our Lord's teaching on the subject of non-retaliation has particularly come under fire. (e.g. Matt. 5:39) Common-sense would suggest that our Lord is not here laying down a principle which could be literally applied in a non-Christian world. The very fact that He recognises the legitimate place of the magistrate and of the law court proves this point. It is clear that He is condemning the spirit of vindictiveness and this particular precept is primarily to be applied in private and personal relationships.

The criticism is sometimes made that the ethical teaching of our Lord, since He lived nearly 2,000 years ago, in a very different environment from our own, cannot possibly be applicable to the modern world. It is contended that the modern man's ethical ideals must be suited to the present age, while the Christian ethic is antiquated and obsolete. Man has now "come of age" and a "new morality" is called for.

In answer to this criticism, it is, of course, conceded that our Lord spoke to His contemporaries and spoke in a language that they could understand. Socrates and Plato and Aristotle did the same. That, however, does not necessarily mean that the principles He laid down were of a merely temporary significance. Human nature is timeless and it is to man as man that the ethical teaching of Jesus is addressed. The main problems of life remain the same. The process of civilisation affects, in the main, only the externals of life. In his internal constitution man is much the same in all ages and in every part of the world. There is nothing that is purely local or transient in the ethical teaching of Jesus. It is adaptable to all nations, to all races, to all types of civilisation and to all conditions. It can never be out of date until man himself is out of date. Although some of the utterances of our Lord had an immediate reference to local and temporary conditions, they also have eternal significance.

The theory was propounded by Johannes Weiss at the beginning of the century, that a great deal of the ethical teaching of Jesus was influenced by His eschatological ideas. Much of it has a special emergency character and was intended for the brief interval of time between His own day and the establishment of the Kingdom. For this reason, some of the demands of our Lord may be regarded as impossible. He called upon men to sever all the ties that bind them to this present world and to make themselves ready for the coming Kingdom. Albert Schweitzer developed this same line of thought. He referred to our Lord as a "world-denier", one whose sole concern was the Kingdom of Heaven. The moral code which He set forth is to be regarded as applicable only to the short intervening period between this present world and the world to come.

This view is based on a misconception of the Kingdom

of God. C. H. Dodd says: "The sayings which declare the kingdom of God to have come are explicit and unequivocal" (e.g. Mark 1:15; Matt. 12:28; Luke 11:20). In point of fact, it is difficult to find a single ethical precept in the Gospels which can be clearly seen to be intended for, and therefore valid only for, a brief interval such as Weiss and Schweitzer mention. When the theory is carefully examined, in the light of our Lord's actual teaching, its absurdity becomes manifest. Besides, the ethical teaching of Jesus does not rest on a merely eschatological foundation and to infer that His ethic is a mere interim-ethic is false. In His ethical teaching, Jesus calls upon men to prepare themselves for the rule of God and promulgates the eternal laws of the Kingdom of God.

Criticism has been levelled at our Lord's teaching on the grounds that He appeals to the idea of reward. (e.g. Matt. 5:12; Matt. 10:41; Matt. 19:27–29). It is contended that this appeal makes motives for goodness selfish and unworthy. Virtue should be sought for virtue's sake, independently of any reward. The higher the level of virtue, the more complete the indifference to all hopes of reward.

While on the face of it such reasoning is plausible, it is not as reasonable as it sounds. There are noble rewards as well as mean ones and there is nothing unethical in the idea that virtue brings a noble reward. Though Joan of Arc and Garibaldi obtained no material reward, they derived infinite satisfaction from the thought that they had served their countries faithfully and that in itself was their reward. There is such a thing as reward which is the natural outcome of a work accomplished even though such a reward may not necessarily be in a tangible form. As the poet Alexander Pope puts it, "What nothing earthly gives or can destroy the soul's colour, sunshine, and the heartfelt joy is virtue's prize; the better you would fix?" In Christian experience, there is such a thing as the joy of service. Our Lord, of course, dismissed the Jewish idea that the pious and the virtuous had a claim on God, for a reward proportionate to their piety and virtue. His parable regarding the vineyard proprietor, who paid all his labourers the same wage, in spite of a variation in their hours of labour, is relevant here. (Matt. 20:1–16) Furthermore, He pointed out that those whose piety was inspired by the desire merely for the esteem of men would get no further reward (Matt. 6:1–5). He counselled men to do good to their fellows without expecting to receive something from them in return by way of reward. (Luke 14:13 ff. and Luke 6:35) It is a plain fact of experience, however, that the pursuit of virtue on the whole leads to pleasure and the pursuit of vice, on the whole, leads to pain. The rewards offered by our Lord are such that only those who are spiritually minded will appreciate them (e.g. Matt. 5:8). In a world governed by God virtue inevitably brings its own reward—not a material reward, but one that is spiritual. If we were living in a universe where virtue brought no such reward and vice no punishment, we should find it difficult to believe in a living God, who is also moral governor of that universe.

In making the point that reward is not the primary consideration in Christian service, we must at the same time be careful not to disparage or deny the promises of God. Our Lord made it clear that God is no man's debtor (Mark 10:30). Whatever compensations Christian self-denial may bring to us in this present life, the fact remains that the Christian hope is basically other-worldly (cf. 1 Cor. 15:19).

The primary motive for Christian obedience, however, is gratitude for the grace of God in Jesus Christ, not reward. Jesus taught that if a man were to seek to gain a reward in this life by his own effort he would forfeit his true reward (Matt. 6:1 ff; Mk. 8:35). Christ laid a much greater emphasis upon sacrifice than reward.

## 6. CHRISTIANITY ACCORDING TO ST. PAUL

Paul, at his conversion, not only gained in the crucified and living Lord a new Master, whom it was his delight to serve, but he also experienced God in a new way. He felt within him the energising power of the Spirit. His transformed religion meant a radically different approach to ethics. Paul's ethical teaching, therefore, can be understood only as it is related to his faith and his experience. For the Apostle, the decisive fact of this Christian experience was that God had revealed His Son to him (Gal. 1:15 ff.). Henceforth he was Christ's willing "slave", belonging to Him, eager at all times to serve Him. In the words "He loved me and gave Himself up for me" (Gal. 2:20) Paul found his supreme inspiration for service. Paul described the Christian experience which was his, not only as life "in Christ" and adoption into sonship, but also as life "in the Spirit". He now relied on the Spirit to produce those fruits which are tokens of Christian character. No longer was he in bondage to the Law; religion ceased to mean the attempt to earn salvation by obedience to commands and prohibitions. Paul sought to meet the needs of those who had been converted from paganism, not by giving them a code of laws, but by urging them to live by the Spirit and bring forth the fruit of the Spirit. Paul constantly based moral exhortation upon religious dogma—this is the general pattern of his

Epistles. The smallest ethical precepts are related to who God is and to what Christ has done: consider, for example, the theological grounds on which Paul urges kindness and forgiveness (Eph. 4:32), humility (Phil. 2:5–11), consideration for others (Rom. 15:3; 1 Cor. 8:11), and brotherly love (Eph. 5:1–2).

Paul's ethical teaching is essentially practical. He registers the results in conduct and character of the life which is based upon faith-union with Christ. The code which, in the form of Jewish law had proved "a law that leads to sin and death" was something from which Christ's disciples had been emancipated. Paul had no intention that another written code should take its place. What had taken its place for the Christian was the "governing principle of the Spirit of life in Christ Jesus" (Rom. 8:2). The interlocking of the religious and the ethical is one of the most characteristic features of Paul's writings; the love which serves is a function of the faith which saves.

Paul set *agape* at the centre of his ethical system. It was the same compelling and controlling force which had moved God to give His Son. Love must be both central and all-comprehensive in the realm of relationships (Gal. 5:14; Rom. 13:8; Col. 3:14). It is the natural self-expression of saving faith and basic to all morals. Christians are essentially those that love God. Love is the basis on which the Church rests, the soil from which it draws its nourishment. In 1 Corinthians chapter 13 Paul sets forth the supremacy of love. This transcendent virtue has actually been poured into the souls of Christians by the Holy Spirit (Romans 5:5). *Agape* sums up for Paul the character of Christ, and is therefore the criterion of Christian conduct. In Paul's thinking faith and love were inseparable (Gal. 5:6). He sees love as the first and greatest fruit of the Spirit.

Paul drew a distinction between the natural man and the spiritual. He contrasts the man who is dominated by the

Spirit with the natural or carnal man who is dominated by his own soul or flesh. Flesh represents the old unregenerate nature—the "old man" (Rom. 6:6; Eph. 4:22–24) which even in a Christian is not completely dead (Col. 3:3 ff.; Rom. 8:13).

Paul teaches that there is a "spirit of man" analogous to the Spirit of God (1 Cor. 2:11), that the regenerate man has received the Spirit of God (1 Cor. 2:12,16; Rom. 8:9), and that this lifts him to an entirely new plane which can be described as "life in the Spirit" rather than "life in the flesh" (Rom. 8:1–11). However, he must walk in the Spirit and be led by the Spirit if he is to bring forth the fruit of the Spirit (Gal. 5:16–25). Moral behaviour is not an unaided human struggle, nor merely the keeping of external laws, but the outcome of the inner effectual working of the Spirit of God. The Holy Spirit is seen as the Christian's ethical dynamic.

Christian ethics is the morality of the regenerate man, and roots the moral life in the putting to death of the soul's natural bias for sin (Eph. 4:20 ff.). The "new man" is a central motif in Pauline ethics (2 Cor. 5:17; Gal. 6:15; Eph. 2:10; 4:24; Col. 3:10; Titus 3:5). Only where supernatural regeneration is experienced is a decisive blow dealt to the old nature (Col. 3:3; Gal. 2:20; 6:14 f.).

The Apostle constantly points out the need for consistency in the lives of Christian people. We are to live as unto Him who has redeemed us (2 Cor. 5:15). If the experience of salvation is real, it will be only natural to care for things which belong to the higher life and to avoid those which belong to the lower (Col. 3:1–8). Paul argued for moral purity on the grounds that the bodies of Christians are temples of the Holy Spirit (1 Cor. 6:18). There must be no self-contradiction in the lives of God's people—Christian conduct ought to be an inevitable result of union with Christ.

Paul constantly emphasized the supremacy of the spiritual side of life with all the ethical implications of this. Paul conceived of the Christian as having in ethical matters a free judgement, which moved within certain wide frontiers defined by the revealed will of God, and, at the same time, was continuously inspired by high examples, and guided by delicate perception of what was "worthy of the Lord", what was becoming in His followers, what was for the good of the Church, and what was seemly in the eyes of men. For the apostle, Christian character and conduct are inseparable, connected with the experience of salvation. Rather than build an ethical system of precepts and prohibitions, Paul deals with problems of conduct as they arise.

Paul claims entire liberty of conscience for each believer in things that are open to question, a liberty which is real, but the exercise of which may be limited by consideration for others (Rom. 14; Col. 2:16–18). Christian liberty is to be used to glorify God and not for sinful indulgence (1 Cor. 10:31; Col. 3:17; Rom. 6:1 ff.).

As already stated, Paul's theology was interlocked with his ethics and his ethics indissolubly bound up with his theology. Like his Master, Paul could not conceive either of unethical religion or of unreligious ethics. He would have agreed with Brunner's statement—"Only ethical religion is truly religious, and only religious ethics is really ethical." And his concern was twofold—to maintain a good conscience (Acts 24:16; 2 Cor. 1:12; 1 Tim. 1:5), and at the same time to be concerned for the tender consciences of others (1 Cor. 8:9; 10:28; Rom. 14).

The Apostle enunciated the general principle that every man should remain in that condition of life in which he was when God called him (1 Cor. 7:21,24). Paul saw a danger in Christianity becoming a movement for social emancipation prematurely. At the same time social relationships at a deeper level were transformed by the fact that they were now "in the Lord". Onesimus still had the status of a slave, but he was also "a brother beloved". (Philemon)

Within marriage a wife's submission to her husband is to be compared with a man's subordination to Christ, and Christ's subordination to God (1 Cor. 11:3; Eph. 5:23). At the same time Christ's love for His Church is to be the standard for a man's love towards his wife (Eph. 5:29). "In Christ" the distinctions of race, social status and sex are in fact transcended (Gal. 3:28).

Children are to "obey their parents in the Lord" (Eph. 6:1; Col. 3:20). Fathers are to refrain from irritating their children (Col. 3:21; cf. Eph. 6:4). Although externally unaltered, the relationship between masters and slaves was transformed when both were "in the Lord". The sting had been drawn from slavery (1 Cor. 7:21,22). Masters are to treat their slaves justly and fairly, and slaves are to obey their masters at every point (Col. 3:22–24; Eph. 6:5–8; 1 Tim. 6:1; Titus 2:9).

Paul teaches that Christians are inter-related as members of the same Body (1 Cor. 12:13; Eph. 4:16). They share common interests and should be concerned for one another (Eph. 4:25–32). They are responsible for encouraging and helping one another (1 Thess. 4:18;5:14).

As regards the world in general Paul corrects a false impression—he rejects as absurd any idea that Christians should isolate themselves from the world (1 Cor. 5:9–12) though they should refrain from inter-marriage with non-Christians (2 Cor. 6:14). Paul is concerned not with flight from the world, but overcoming the world by the indwelling power of the Spirit of God. In civil affairs, Christians are to pay due regard to the government, meeting its demands (Rom. 13:1–7).

As we have seen, Paul's direct ethical teaching is limited to general principles, or to those particular problems to which his attention was called. He saw the hopelessness of attempting to obey a moral law prior to or apart from faith-union with Christ. He was not an ethical philosopher, for he entered into no discussion of ethical theories. His ethical interest was purely practical, and in his letters there are scores of ethical exhortations dealing with matters that should be obvious to the Christian—even including such an elementary ethical law as "Let the stealer steal no more". (Eph. 4:28) He was concerned simply and solely with the results in character and conduct of that union with Christ, which for him was the central feature of Christian experience.

Although unmarried himself, Paul did not condemn marriage. His motive in urging celibacy was not the suspicion that marriage was unclean, but the desire that in view of the seriousness of the times people should be spared the burden of family responsibilities (1 Cor. 7:28, 32). Indeed, he seems to have regarded celibacy as a "charisma" from God, while at the same time regarding the married state as normal. In sexual matters, as in other departments of life, he stressed the need for self-discipline for the Christian (1 Cor. 9:25ff), for the body is a good servant but a bad master, and needs discipline. He does not stress this because he is by nature an ascetic, but because it is practical and sensible.

Paul constantly insisted that no law or code was adequate for the ethical needs of man. Morality is not a matter of mere rules and regulations. The real human tragedy is not one of ignorance of what is right, but of impotence to do right. A code can prescribe what a man ought to do, but cannot dispose him to do it. Goodness, Paul taught, was not something that men achieved for themselves, but is the gift of God's grace (Gal. 3:25). The Law had brought home to men their real condition, and held up before them an ideal which they were obliged to confess they were unable to reach (Rom. 7:7 ff.). Paul sums up the position in the words, "For the code kills, but the Spirit makes alive" (2 Cor. 3:6). When a man commits himself to God in Christ his spirit comes under the sway of the divine Spirit, and that Spirit is the source and spring of a new life and work in his heart. Through the Spirit a man is gripped by divine power, so that his disposition is changed and he wills increasingly what God wills. The Spirit brings man power to do the will of God, while a mere code is powerless. The Christian's moral life is not a human attempt to obey a law, but is the fruit of a divine Spirit dwelling within him. Faith in Christ was for Paul the primary ethical requirement.

Although Paul repudiated the code-method of morality he recognised that moral principles embodied in the law of Moses were still binding, so that the Christian is not without law (see Rom. 8:4,8; 1 Cor. 9:12). The Christian life is therefore a controlled, ordered, disciplined service, a service which nevertheless is "perfect freedom" (1 Cor. 7:22) even though it calls for strenuous moral effort and self-discipline—it is significant that the Christian is pictured as both soldier (2 Tim. 2:4) and athlete (1 Cor. 9:24–27; 2 Tim. 2:5).

As Barclay so aptly reminds us: "The Pauline ethic may be nineteen hundred years old, but it is still as valid as ever, and not even yet have its implications been completely worked out."

# 7. MARRIAGE AND DIVORCE

Brunner in his book *Justice and the Social Order* declares, "Every state will learn by experience that it cannot allow the Divine order of creation to be infringed with impunity. All political anarchy in the state begins with anarchy in marriage. The state in which adultery and divorce are the order of the day is also ripe for political decay... If the social basis, marriage, is rotten the whole community is rotten."

Marriage is seen in Scripture as an order of creation (Genesis 1:27; 2:24; Matt. 19:4–5)—the two sexes by God's intention and design belong together (1 Cor. 11:11). Marriage and the family are not social conveniences discovered by man, but exist by God's ordination and appointment. While Moses "for the hardness of men's hearts" had allowed divorce, this was contrary to the original divine intention. There would, as our Lord pointed out, always be those who for the sake of God's kingdom might renounce marriage, but marriage itself was a noble estate. (Matt. 19:12; Heb. 13:4) The Old Testament pattern for marriage was a written agreement publicly witnessed, followed by private committal. The agreement was settled by gifts between the families concerned (e.g. Gen. 29:18; Ruth 3:15) and the wedding was associated with certain ceremonies (Mark 2:9; Matt. 25:1–13). A betrothal was a legal contract only to be broken by a formal divorce.

Marriage is the God-ordained means whereby the human race is perpetually renewed (Gen. 1:28). God permits man to share derivatively in the work of creation. The family is the God-given unit, not only for the procreation of children but also for their nurture (Psalm 127:3; Eph. 6:4). Marriage is, furthermore, an outlet for the expression of natural sexual desire, and, negatively, it may be seen as a safeguard against sin (1 Cor. 7:2,9,36; 1 Thess. 4:3–5). In a word, marriage is a divinely ordained way by which men and women satisfy physical and emotional needs and provide for the continuation of society.

The apostle Paul compared the relation of husband and wife to the relationship between Christ and the Church (Eph. 5:22 ff.). The fact that such comparison should be made bears witness to the lofty conception of marriage which was held in the early Church.

In the New Testament Christ is represented as the Bridegroom (Mark 2:19; Jn. 3:29), in the reality of whose presence the Church rejoices. The Old Testament idea of Israel as Jehovah's spouse (cf. Hosea 3; Isa. 54; Jer. 3; Ezek. 16) is given a Christian application by the apostle Paul when he writes to the Corinthians (2 Cor. 11:2). The final blessedness of the consummation of the age is represented under the symbol of the marriage feast (Matt. 25:1–13; Rev. 19:9). A Church which could so naturally turn to the marriage metaphor for the expression of its deepest theological insights is obviously a Church in which the institution of marriage is regarded with the highest degree of veneration. We recall also that our Lord attended in person a wedding feast at the commencement of His ministry (Jn. 2:1–11).

Marriage is a contract between two parties protected by law. It involves a total claim of two persons on each other, not to be broken until the death of one partner (Matt. 5:32). Christian marriage differs from the natural institution by the fact that a third Person is involved; it is marriage "in the Lord"—a contract in which the grace of God is available for its fulfilment.

Marriage is not necessarily the particular will of God for each one of His children (Matt. 19:10–12). Some choose to remain single so that they may better serve God (1 Cor. 7:27,32–33; 35, etc.). Nowhere does the Bible state that a man or a woman's sole destiny is in marriage and parenthood. No one accepts the call to celibacy without finding God's gifts multiplied to them in other ways. Each one has his own special "charisma". (1 Cor. 7:7).

While before God there is equality of status between men and women (Gal. 3:28) there remains a difference of function (1 Cor. 11:3). The nature of man's headship is defined by reference to the work of Christ (Eph. 5:23–25). The relationship between Christ and the Church is archetypal for Christian marriage. Every man is to "love his wife even as himself", and every woman is to "reverence her husband" (Eph. 5:33). Sexual relationships are to be governed by responsibility and mutual consideration, both husband and wife having definite and equal sexual needs which are to be met within marriage. (1 Cor. 7:2,3,4,5)

The apostle Paul found nothing wrong in contracting a second marriage. Although he advised widows to remain unmarried, he conceded that they were perfectly free to remarry provided they married a Christian partner (1 Cor. 7:39). He condemned mixed marriages (2 Cor. 6:14).

Divorce was only too common in the ancient world; women were considered as chattels with no legal rights. Seneca remarked "Women are married to be divorced and divorced to be married."

In Judaism, however, the preservation of the family was all-important, and this sometimes led to a double standard of morality whereby higher virtue was demanded from the wife than from the husband, chastity not being always considered obligatory upon the man. But as time went on greater emphasis was placed on the sanctity of marriage as a lifelong union. According to the Talmud it was not permissible for a woman to take the initiative in seeking a divorce. While the validity of divorce was recognised its abuse was prevented by moral injunction and judicial regulation. By the time of Christ there was a sharp division of opinion between the rivals schools of Rabbi Shammai and Rabbi Hillel over the interpretation of the Deuteronomic phrase "some matter of uncleanness" (Deut. 24:1,2). Shammai restricted the right of divorce to the case of an unchaste wife, whereas Hillel argued that a husband had the right of divorce on almost any grounds, such as going out with her hair in disarray, talking to another man or being a nagging wife.

As we have seen, Christians differed as to whether Christ's injunctions are intended as an inexorable law for His followers, to which there can be no exception, an ideal standard to which they should aspire, or something in between the two. A clue to this problem is provided in a passage dealing with this very question of divorce, where someone puts to Jesus a similar question about the injunctions of Moses.

When asked whether divorce was permissible for every cause, our Lord replied that Moses permitted it by way of concession because of the hardness of men's hearts, but that divorce was not part of the original order of creation, but a concession to man in his fallen state (Matt. 19:8). Considerable discussion has taken place regarding the words "except for fornication" (Matt. 19:9). Some have thought that this refers to pre-marital unchastity discovered after marriage (Deut. 22:13–21) while others regard it as referring to unfaithfulness in marriage. Some have even suggested that it might be a later insertion into the text of some manuscripts to tone down the rigorous nature of our Lord's teaching.

There are today those Christians who hold that since marriage is a life-long union it can only be broken by the death of one or other of the contracting parties, and that divorce can therefore be countenanced under no circumstances. Others regard a dissolved marriage, like the breaking of any other solemn vow, as a sin dishonouring to God but believe that marriage can no longer be held to exist when the contract which made the marriage has been broken. It is difficult to see how a human relationship which has been irrevocably terminated can continue to exist in any meaningful sense as a theological abstraction. Paul's remark that "God has called us to peace" (1 Cor. 7:15) would suggest that there are situations in which to try to preserve a marriage would only lead to impossible tension and frustration and this can hardly be according to God's will.

The phrase "Pauline privilege" is sometimes used of the Apostle's ruling here. In cases where the unbeliever in a mixed marriage is no longer willing to live with his believing partner and takes the initiative in separating from her, the deserted wife is no longer bound by the marriage and presumably is therefore free to remarry. The Apostle acknowledges that on some of these points he has no direct word from Christ, but he assures his readers that he believes he has the Spirit of God (1 Cor. 7:12,40). Ideally, however, Christians, even if married to unbelievers, are called upon to uphold the sanctity of marriage and avoid seeking divorce (1 Cor. 7:10,11).

While the New Testament, then, clearly teaches that divorce should be exceptional, it does not teach that it is impossible. However, easy divorce in effect turns every marriage into a trial marriage. Those who argue for divorce by consent do so on the grounds of the basic principle of freedom of moral judgement: the parties concerned should be free to end it like any other contract when they wish. But they ignore the far reaching social consequences of a broken marriage. For a Christian even adultery should not necessarily be regarded as an automatic reason for divorce. It is virtually impossible to impose the full Christian ethic on a "mixed" society, Christians, however, have a God-given responsibility to try to convince their fellow-citizens of the relevance and importance of those principles which they believe to be essential to the well-being of society and of its individual members.

In Britain, the Divorce Act of 1857 restricted divorce to adultery by the wife, or adultery and cruelty in the husband. The Matrimonial Causes Act of 1937 permitted divorce not only for cruelty and incurable insanity, but for three years or more of desertion. The Lambeth Conference of 1948 declared, "We are bound to admit that a union indissoluble by Divine institution may in fact be wrecked by sin." A more recent Archbishop's Commission on Divorce recommended that the doctrine of "the breakdown of marriage" be comprehensively substituted for the doctrine of the matrimonial offence as the basis of all divorce. It is claimed that a divorce founded on the doctrine of breakdown would have the merit of showing up divorce for what it essentially is: "Not a reward for marital virtue on the one side and a penalty for marital delinquency on the other; not a victory for one spouse and a reverse for the other, but a defeat for both, a failure of the marital 'two-in-oneship' in which both its members, however unequal their responsibility, are inevitably involved together." It is further claimed that this new concept would give greater prominence to the question of reconciliation.

The Commission also recommended that the power of the court to insist on satisfactory arrangements being made for the children should be retained, and if possible strengthened, and that the rights of the unoffending wife who may be divorced against her will should be the subject of special safeguards. The Lord Chancellor's Law Commission declared that these proposals would choke the administration of justice and cause hardship and endless delay. The proposal of the Commission was that husband and wife should be in a position to petition for divorce on the ground that there has been a breakdown, and that there should be "divorce by consent".

To sum up the legal position in Britain—the basis of Divorce Law up to comparatively recently has been "the matrimonial offences". More recent legislation has replaced this by "the breakdown of the marriage". A court is now able to infer that a marriage has broken down if one of five grounds is proved—adultery, a period of 3 years' desertion by either party, cruelty, a period of 2 years lived apart with both parties desiring divorce, or 5 years apart if only one party wants the divorce. This means, in effect, that even if one party does not want a divorce at the end of the five years they are forced to accept it.

In the face of mounting divorce figures in the Western world the Christian Church is being called upon as never before to underline the sanctity of marriage. We need to recall that the first century Christians were concerned to maintain their high ideals against a background of permissiveness and promiscuity no less pronounced than that of our time. It could not have been easy for those early Christians to escape the moral infection of their day, and inevitably, because of the frailty of human nature, there were some casualties then as there are today. But in no sense is the Church permitted to lower its ideal of marriage as a life-long union between husband and wife. In cases where, through sin and selfishness, marriages have broken up without hope of repair, Christian people are called upon to exercise a ministry of compassion and not merely to condemn.

## 8. LOVE AND SEX

An article in *Time Magazine* made this comment: "The Victorians, who talked a great deal about love, knew little about sex. Perhaps it is time that modern Americans, who know a great deal about sex, once again start talking about love."

Sex and love are not identical, since sex is primarily a physical response while love is primarily a response of one's inner being. There is an absence of true love when a man or woman is used simply as an instrument to satisfy strong physical or emotional desires.

The Christian attitude to sex is supremely one of reverent responsibility. Men and women cannot indulge in sexual relationships without affecting their whole natures. Sex relations outside marriage violate the scriptural analogy of Christ and the Church. True love demands the complete surrender of each to the other, which is only possible within the framework of marriage. Fornication is the selfish satisfaction of the urge to physical union, sometimes without regard for the consequences, and without admitting the necessity for a covenant to safeguard the relationship. (1 Cor. 6:18) Trial or companionate marriage is a relationship without any sense of permanence or security. It is of the essence of marriage that it shall be stable, and it is only in the assurance of such stability that lives truly grow together.

Sex before marriage is the demand for privilege without responsibility, for rights without commitment.

Within marriage there must be both mutual respect and self-control. Abstinence must be by mutual consent, temporary in nature and for a sufficiently good reason. Generally speaking, lengthy abstinence or separation is to be avoided, although special circumstances might make it necessary. Husbands and wives have a responsibility to meet each other's sexual needs. (1 Cor. 7:2–5)

Prostitution is contrary to the laws of human relationships. It endangers the health of the community and causes psychological damage to both men and women. It debases human personality, reducing men to the level of animals. Promiscuity assumes that sexual fulfilment can be achieved at a superficial level of personal relationship without total commitment and the responsibilities that go with it. It is a negation of love because it divorces the physical act from the context in which alone it finds its sanctity and meaning. The prostitute exploits the lust of her clients and they in turn exploit the moral weakness of the prostitute.

If fornication becomes the accepted pattern of life in any society the logical consequence is that men and women lose respect for each other as persons.

Let us now look at the question of birth control or family planning. It was not until 1934 that birth control methods were made at all public and then only to a very limited extent. There was, of course, always abstinence, which the Scriptures say is advisable only for limited periods (1 Cor. 7:5) though in itself it is ethically permissible. The crucial question is whether it is permissible to limit child-bearing by artificial methods. Birth control alleviates the problem of the unwanted child. It also places upon the parents the solemn responsibility of deciding when their children shall be born. In this question, our point of reference should be that reverence for human life which lies at the heart of Christian ethics. For this very reason the Roman Catholic Church regards limitations on child-bearing in marriage as exceptional, and only to be occasioned either by sexual continence or by the "natural rhythm" method. Use of unnatural or mechanical devices stands condemned by papal decree. Here we may well ask whether the use of so-called mechanical methods is more "unnatural" than the rhythm method. Contraception has found its peak in "the Pill"—which from some points of view appears to be less "unnatural" and, of course, far simpler to use, than many other methods.

Dr. F. R. Barry, a former Bishop of Southwell wrote in his book, *Christian Ethics and Secular Society*, "Deliberate prevention of conception is necessary in the normal marriage. It follows that to deny to married couples the use of contraceptives must result either in the conception of children in wrong circumstances, or in the risks that follow indefinite abstention from sexual intercourse." It must be stressed of course that birth control, unlike abortion, is concerned not with destroying life but with preventing its beginning. Furthermore, it should be recognized that to make any attempt, however crude or futile, to minimise the chances of conception, is to practise some form of birth control.

A topic of current debate is the advisability or otherwise of providing contraceptive advice for unmarried people. Whereas to do this would appear to be encouraging promiscuity, the tragic alternatives all too often are not between chastity and contraceptive advice, but between sexual relationships outside marriage, with all the attendant risks and the safeguards which such advice can provide. The wholesale distribution of contraceptives to the unmarried, however, cannot be approved by Christian people. Furthermore, the question has to be faced whether a Christian doctor in giving "the pill" to an unmarried girl is not in fact condoning illicit sexual activity.

We shall now consider the matter of abortion. By this

we mean the expulsion of a living foetus from the uterus before its life can be maintained apart from the mother. The question arises here whether the sanctity of human life extends back before birth, and if so, how far. Is a foetus always to be regarded at all stages as a living entity? There is no scriptural warrant for claiming that God regards the foetus as equivalent to a life (cf. Exod. 21:22–24). Nevertheless it is God who is actively involved in the process of fashioning the foetus (Ps. 139:13–18). All Christians are agreed that men must not take life, yet there will always be cases in which it seems right from a Christian standpoint to terminate a pregnancy. Therapeutic abortion, where there are extenuating circumstances, and with due medical safeguards, is now permissible in law. The problem of abortion may involve weighing the claims of the mother against those of the unborn child. Recent legislation in Britain means that basically an abortion can now be carried out if any two doctors agree that the pregnancy would affect the physical or mental health of the mother or seriously overstrain her. Such a decision involves taking into account the "total environment", social and medical, of the woman and her family. An abortion is now legal if there is substantial risk that the child would be born seriously handicapped, mentally or physically, or if the woman is a defective, or became pregnant under the age of 16 or as a result of rape.

In dealing with this complex issue we must accept that human life is sacrosanct and that the potentialities of an unborn child are unknown. Apart from Roman Catholics, most Christians take the view that where the issue is between the life of the unborn child and that of the mother, the mother has the prior claim since she has immediate responsibilities to her husband and any children. The so-called "social clause" in the recent Abortion Bill is clearly open to abuse and its value is highly questionable.

Sterilization of the unfit is another topic which should be mentioned. Apart from the case of parents infected with venereal disease there is no evidence that the children of poor, ill-nourished or overworked parents, or of parents living in bad conditions, are at birth in any way inferior to the average child. In the case of parents definitely suffering from hereditary disease a strong case could be made for sterilization for the protection of society. Any attempt, however, at compulsory sterilization involves an infringement of human rights, and a violation of personal freedom and dignity which the Christian is bound to condemn and resist. Therapeutic sterilization by consent is covered by the same principles applicable to therapeutic abortion.

Artificial human insemination is yet another topic in current debate. Christian opinion generally condemns artificial insemination by a donor (A.I.D.) as being a deliberate violation of the marital relationship. The donor is making himself a party to what is morally an adulterous relationship. When, however, normal conception is impossible most Christians would feel there can be no moral objection to artificial insemination by the husband (A.I.H.). Some would countenance A.I.D. if this was with the husband's consent and would question whether the term adultery was applicable in a situation where the parties concerned had never met.

Homosexuality is a further issue which should be considered from a Christian point of view. It has been stated that of the first fifteen Roman Emperors, fourteen were practising homosexuals—so it can scarcely be called a modern problem! We apply the term "inversion" to the diversion of the psycho-sexual impulse more or less exclusively towards persons of the same sex by those who should have reached psycho-sexual maturity. Some authorities contend that human beings pass through a stage of relative homosexuality in their progress from childhood to maturity. One of the most frequent causes of permanent inversion is an unsatisfactory emotional adjustment in childhood. The Wolfenden Report accepted the view that there exists in certain persons a homosexual propensity, and that homosexual behaviour between consenting adults in private should no longer be a criminal offence. A clear distinction must be made between homosexuality and homosexual acts—homosexual activities as distinct from inclinations cannot be justified.

The Bible is emphatic in its condemnation of all homosexual acts (Gen. 19:1–11; Lev. 18:22; 20:13; Rom. 1:27; I Cor. 6:9,19; I Tim. 1:8–11). Augustine condemned what he called "shameful acts against nature". With our strong denunciation of sin, however, there must always be compassion for the sinner. While many would agree that the law earlier against sexual offences was savage, one fears that more recent legislation would appear to condone sexual perversion. The issue is whether the fact of inversion should be approached as a clinical or a moral question. Even though it has far-reaching moral implications it is today widely accepted that the mere fact of being, congenitally or from whatever cause, a sex invert is not in itself a matter for moral judgement though it calls for a great deal of moral help. It is generally conceded that perversion on a large scale is a symptom of a degenerate society. In any society the extent of homosexual practices and perversion is always one of the most striking indications of a general corruption or defect in its sexual life.

To sum up: as Christians, we see homosexual practices as sins and contrary to nature but we must recognize that it is virtually impossible for legal action to be enforced without continual intrusion into people's privacy. We must be careful to distinguish between homosexuality and homosexual acts. Furthermore, in condemning the sin, we must not fail to have compassion on the sinner.

At the present time the whole area of sex ethics is one of considerable debate in Christian circles. There are those in positions of leadership who even question whether chastity should be extolled as a virtue and taught to young people. Some would go so far as to represent our Lord as being a champion of the permissive society, But no one can honestly examine the teaching of the New Testament without coming to the conclusion, however reluctantly, that such indulgences as fornication and sexual intercourse outside marriage are wholly wrong, as adultery is wrong. If we are to maintain any real relationship with New Testament Christianity then we must as Christians take our stand clearly and unequivocally for sexual purity. As Sherwin Bailey in *Sexual Ethics* points out, "However imperfectly they grasped them, however ineffectually they put them into practice, Christians recognized from the first that certain sexual truths belonged to the Gospel—the spiritual equality of men and women in the sight of God, the high theological significance of marriage, the impartial application of the rule of chastity to both sexes."

# 9. RESPECT FOR LIFE

In this chapter we shall be looking at several issues which relate to the sanctity of human life and personality.

Until the turn of the present century the word "euthanasia" was applied solely to the alleviation of the sufferings of the dying. It was not used as a synonym for "mercy-killing". The current idea of euthanasia, of hastening the death of someone from motives of compassion, covers two main situations:—where someone is close to death and can be kept alive for a few more hours or days only by the most intensive medical care; or where someone may be expected to live for perhaps weeks, months or even years, but in considerable pain or in such circumstances that life, it would seem, is not worth living.

Modern medical science is able to prolong substantially the life of a patient who is near death. The question is whether to keep alive a person who by normal considerations has reached the end of his or her life-span, and who would not continue to live except by the use of extensive and exceptional medical techniques. It may legitimately be argued that we never know that there is no hope of at least a brief and perhaps partial recovery, in which case every effort should be made to keep the patient alive. Certainly it seems morally indefensible to bring to an end the life of, say, a spastic child by deliberately refusing, for example, to administer antibiotics during an attack of pneumonia. In his book *Morals in a Free Society* Keeling writes: "The facts of disablement provide no grounds for saying that there is any level at which life is not worth living. Those who believe that some human beings can be written off, and that they are in a position to judge who they should be, are treading a dangerous road, at the end of which we can all be devalued." All branches of the Christian Church agree in condemning "mercy killing". Life is not at the absolute disposal of the holder, but is a gift from God and lies in His control.

From the medical point of view it must be understood that prognosis may be mistaken, and that some diseases clear up for no known reason. Also, the practice of euthanasia would undermine the relationship between patient and doctor. At present English law refuses to countenance any form of euthanasia. Doctors or others who assist sick persons to end their lives are, in the eyes of the law, guilty of a criminal offence. Were euthanasia ever legalized there would be a number of abuses and problems which would inevitably arise. Allowances must be made, for example, for the patient's own fluctuations of mood. The patient might apply for euthanasia in a passing fit of despair. There is also the danger of coercion on the part of relatives who tire of the problems of nursing the patient. Even if we ourselves discern no useful purpose in remaining alive, it is in effect a denial of God's providence to take the law into our own hands, and elect to end our own or someone else's life. The medical practitioner must seek to pursue an essentially positive role, whilst mitigating the suffering of those in his care.

When the case has been rightly and properly made against euthanasia, one is nevertheless bound to question whether it is necessarily the will of God to use modern drugs and advanced medical techniques to bring an elderly person with an apparently incurable disease back to a state of mere existence. Because the Bible forbids a man to take his own life or that of another, we must not necessarily conclude that a doctor is duty bound to prolong life indefinitely by the use of elaborate and expensive means when life for the patient concerned has ceased to be meaningful in any real sense. In the words of A. H. Clough:

> "Thou shalt not kill: but need'st not strive
> Officiously to keep alive."

Now let us turn to another related topic—suicide.

The suicide is the product of a society which has made him feel that life is no longer worthwhile, and it is a significant fact that the suicide rate is highest in countries which have the highest standards of living. In English law suicide was for a long time regarded as a criminal offence, although comparatively few prosecutions were instigated for attempting it. The Homicide Act of 1957 reduced the charge in a suicide pact from murder to manslaughter. The primary concern of Christian thinking should be with the underlying social causes of suicide and with the pastoral and psychiatric approaches to it.

The fundamental Christian objection to suicide rests on the grounds that life is God's gift, and we have no right to reject it; the bounds of life belong to God alone. Suicide in Scripture seems to symbolise the despair of reprobate men as in the case of Saul and Judas Iscariot. In any formulation of a Christian judgement it has to be remembered that "suicide" is a term that covers a variety of acts which differ widely in moral quality. There is, for example, all the difference in the world between the case of a man who throws himself across his wife's body to shield her from an explosion or a rifle shot, and someone else who takes "the easy way out" because he cannot face the consequences of some crime which he has committed. In certain countries of the East self-immolation has been regarded as heroic, but Semitic religions have consistently discountenanced suicide. The Rabbis forbid it to the Jews in all circumstances, and Moslems say that to kill oneself is the worst kind of murder. Greek moralists generally speaking condemned suicide, but the Romans were divided on the subject. The Stoics, for example, extolled suicide as the appointed means of escape from all kinds of misery. Thomas Aquinas described suicide as the most fatal of sins because it cannot be repented of. In modern times suicide is more common among men than women, among the unmarried than the married, among the childless than those who have children, and among the young and middle-aged than the old. A growing suicide rate is a clear symptom of a sick society.

Those blessed with good health, creative jobs and happy homes are sometimes too ready to condemn out of hand the person who has been tempted to take his own life. Few Christians are happy simply to dismiss suicide as a crime. The strains and stresses of life, broken homes, the incidence of incurable disease and many other factors may drive a man or woman who has no refuge to the brink of despair. Even professing Christians overcome by depressive illnesses have been known to take their own lives. Clearly, in such cases due consideration must be given to the circumstances.

We shall glance now at one or two issues raised by fairly recent developments in the field of medical science.

Transplant surgery poses a number of ethical problems, particularly in the case of heart or brain transplants where obviously the donor must die before his organ can be attached to another body.

Since doctors generally no longer find the point of death in heart arrest or absence of respiration, but rather in absence of brain function, some prospective heart donors may be illegally considered "dead". Have not some patients recovered after temporary cessation of heart function and led normal lives?

Brain transplants, if they ever become practicable, would involve more complicated problems than heart transplants. In view of the intimate connection between brain and character, the question arises: who survives in a brain transplant, the donor or the recipient? Does this issue affect the question of personal moral responsibility and accountability to God? However, the possibility of such transplants seems so remote that these questions are hypothetical at present.

The border-line between accepted and experimental procedures in surgery is not always easy to draw. Inescapable responsibility rests upon the doctor to ensure that what he is about to do is, in fact, in the best interests of his patient. Any medical or surgical action has to have the consent of the patient or someone authorized to act on his behalf. The removal of any of the organs of a deceased person can only take place if this was (or is) the expressed wish of that person and/or is agreed by the surviving relatives. Any doctor involved in transplant surgery should satisfy himself that the parties concerned have been given all the necessary knowledge and complete freedom to decide whether they agree to this particular course of action. Furthermore, it should be possiblc to assume that the proposed operation is such that the doctor would advise it in the case of someone near and dear to him, or such that he would wish it done for himself in similar circumstances.

Scientific research proceeds at an incredible pace. Medical science now claims to be able to change human personality—to be able to alter the genes in an ovum. Whereas this is to be welcomed if it prevents the passing on of congenital physical deformities it is clearly open to abuse, and needs the most careful safeguards. It could be said that a scientist sets out to alter a personality via the genes and a Christian by the gospel. But is such a comparison valid? Changing the genes may affect temperament and certain characteristics, but only Christ can create a "new man" and at the same time deal with the matter of human guilt. Too much can be made of the influence of genes on behaviour. We must not forget the part played by education and environment in the development of human life. The science of neuropharmacology also opens up the possibility of changing people's personalities through drugs, and this, too, is fraught with dangers.

From a Christian point of view the dignity of human personality is always to be upheld. Christianity takes its stand on the fact that man is made in the image of God and must be respected as an individual in his own right. Furthermore there is always the underlying Christian assumption of life after death—"If for this life only we have hoped in Christ, we are of all men most to be pitied" (1 Cor. 15:19). It is open to question whether the preservation of life on this earth *at all costs* is justifiable from a Christian point of view. After all, the length of a man's earthly life is not an end in itself, and "what shall it profit a man if he shall gain the whole world and lose his own soul?"

## 10. THE CHRISTIAN AND WORK

The Bible makes it clear that it is the will of God that men should work (Genesis 2:15): work is a creation ordinance. The first allusion to the institution of labour after the fall of man is in the curse pronounced upon Adam (Genesis 3:17–19). It should be noted that the curse is not the curse of labour as such; it is the pain of hardship connected with labour, and the frustration that men will encounter by reason of the curse upon the ground. The earliest and simplest form of work is agriculture, since the production of food is basic to life—"Abel was a keeper of sheep, but Cain a tiller of the ground" (Genesis 4:2). The natural resources of the world were created by God and were given to man to use and develop. (Genesis 1:26).

In the Decalogue we read—"Six days you shall labour and do all your work". (Exodus 20:9) Consistently throughout the Scriptures we find the idea of earning one's living by honest work commended (Psalm 128:2; I Thessalonians 2:9; II Thessalonians 3:7 ff. etc.). Work is regarded as the inevitable and necessary lot of mankind (Psalm 104:19–23). The Book of Proverbs abounds in exhortations to industry and warnings against idleness (e.g. Proverbs 6:6). Some of the most bitter denunciations uttered by the prophets were directed against the idle rich (e.g. Amos 6:3–6). The Hebrews saw work not as something degrading but a normal part of the divine ordering of the world. It should not be beneath the dignity even of a king to work with his hands. (I Samuel 11:5) Paul aimed to preach the gospel without being paid because he felt that in this way his witness would be more effective. Furthermore, he desired to preserve his independence and self-respect, and, by his example, to give his converts a lesson in diligence and self-reliance. He urged his converts to follow his example and to work not only in their own interests, but that they might be in a position to assist others who were in need (Ephesians 4:28). He saw honest labour as a way of commending the gospel. (I Thessalonians 4:11). He dealt sternly with fanatics at Thessalonica who were so sure that the Parousia was at hand that they had given up working and consequently had to live on other people. (II Thessalonians 3:10 ff.).

According to the Apostle, no man was worthy of the name of Christ unless he was eager both to support himself and to help others by honest work, provided he was physically able to work. A Christian does not work simply to make money, or to pay bills, but because it is part of the divine order that he should work. It is the duty of the Christian to use his God-given abilities to the limit of his physical and mental capacity. Christians glorify God before an unbelieving world by pointing to the kind of life which God intended man to live. It is clear from the Scriptures that man was intended to control and put to use the untamed resources of the world, and for this he was given powers of intellect and organisation. The Christian is therefore taught to regard work as a divine vocation.

To do one's work well is to be in a position to receive the blessing of God—happy is the man whose labour is blessed by God (Psalm 128:2), and wretched is he whose toil is not so blessed (Isaiah 62:8; 65:23).

Since work is the common lot of mankind, and is in fact a divine ordinance for the life of man, it should be undertaken cheerfully and without complaint. When we are conscious of divine vocation in the particular task assigned to us, we will have the proper sense of responsibility in the discharge of it (I Corinthians 10:31; Colossians 3:17); if we are not ready to work for the good of the community, insufficient work will be done and economic stability endangered.

"As serving the Lord and not men" should sum up the Christian's attitude towards his work. (Colossians 3:22, 23). Whatever his work is he must do it with enthusiasm and not grudgingly, or because he is driven to it. Not only must a Christian work, but he must work as if for God, and he must work whole-heartedly (I Thessalonians 4:11, 12; Ecclesiastes 9:10). Work is to be done well (Colossians 3:23,24). Since all work is done for Christ, we must put our best into it. We must avoid becoming mere men-pleasers (Colossians 3:22; Ephesians 6:5–8). The conception of the divine dignity of work is distinctive in Hebrew and Christian teaching. Luther and the Reformers did great service in re-affirming the Christian view of the sanctity of work.

It is quite wrong for Christians to despise certain kinds of work as being inferior to others. We find no sense of contempt for manual labour in the New Testament. Our Lord Himself did the work of an artisan. (Mark 6:3) Paul worked with his hands as a tentmaker. There are comparatively few occupations which are immoral in themselves, and therefore which a Christian should avoid. Among these occupations which a Christian may hesitate to enter, we might include those in which what is provided for public consumption is likely to do positive harm in present conditions. We might also include occupations which, while not obviously doing positive harm, are not providing any useful service to society, or occupations, permissible in themselves, into which a Christian should not enter because of some known weakness in his character.

In the case of most occupations, however, what matters for the Christian is the way in which the occupation is carried out rather than the nature of the occupation itself.

Man, made in the image of God, has a right to life, and must therefore have the right to work in order to maintain that life. Enforced idleness denies that right and leads to a lowering of morale and has inevitable effects on the family structure.

Some economists argue that a certain degree of unemployment provides an incentive to work and makes for a greater mobility of labour, yet unemployment is a social evil which the Christian cannot condone though he may have to accept in an imperfect society. Unemployment prevents a man from using his natural powers in the way God meant he should. The Biblical principle was that all are entitled to food, shelter and clothes, but not without work. (II Thessalonians 3:10) Whatever a man's or woman's position in life may be, it is against the divine intention that days should be spent in idleness.

The New Testament, upholding the fourth Commandment, also recognises the need of and right to leisure. Our Lord emphasised the Sabbath as being a day of rest and recreation for toiling men. (Mark 2:27–28). There is, in the natural order of things, as symbolised in the days of creation, a rhythm of work and rest. In the New Testament, rest is spoken of as the proper culmination of man's work on earth. In the Mosaic Law the command to observe the Sabbath belongs not merely to the ritual sections of that Law abrogated by the gospel, but also to the Decalogue. A weekly day of rest is a rule imposed from the beginning by the Creator upon all men. On this day there was to be a cessation from buying and selling to make money. (Amos 8:5). Regular physical rest is seen as being necessary for true health and well-being, to men and beasts alike. (Exodus 23:12; Deut. 5:14). Christ Himself asserted the perpetuity of this creation ordinance. (Mark 2:27).

The two main threats to a day of rest in the modern world are shift work and employment necessitated by the pleasure and convenience of others. Where shift work is manifestly the fruit of industrial covetousness, and does not arise from some intrinsic factor in the work itself, it should be resisted, and at the same time every effort made to reduce the volume of non-essential employment on this day.

From the Scriptures, therefore, we conclude that work is at once a fundamental right and duty. Furthermore, a weekly day of rest is both a biological and a spiritual necessity.

One of the unresolved problems which will have to be faced by future generations is how to teach men and women to make the best use of their leisure hours. In the modern world the working week tends to become shorter and shorter, but few people seem to be equipped to put their spare time to good use. The Christian no doubt has fewer problems here than most, since he is under a very definite obligation to "redeem the time". The Roman world faced the same sort of problem as we shall be facing. At one time there were some 150,000 people in Rome with no work to do, and a further 100,000 whose work lasted only till mid-day. Juvenal suggested that all the people were really interested in was "bread and circuses". The people gave themselves up to such pleasures as gambling, chariot-racing, the gladiatorial games, and blood sports of one kind and another. They were not trained to make good use of their leisure hours with the result that society degenerated morally and spiritually. Twentieth-century man is also in danger of having more leisure hours than he knows how to put to good use.

Boredom is quickly becoming one of the major problems of our society. Increasing juvenile delinquency bears witness to this fact. We are facing a situation in which men and women need education for leisure. Christian people will wish to use their influence to discourage men and women from forms of pleasure and relaxation which may have harmful effects on the person who indulges in them, or on others. Ideally, leisure pursuits should be directed to the best interests of the whole man—relaxing the body, refreshing the mind, and at the same time recognising the needs of the spirit.

# 11. CHRISTIANITY AND MODERN INDUSTRY

Like the prophets before Him (see Isaiah 5:7,8; Micah 3:1–3; Amos 5:24), our Lord denounced the combination of religious profession and social injustice. (Matt. 23:14). He spoke in strong condemnation of those who "devour widows' houses, who oppress the poor and the defenceless", and yet claim to be religious men. A Christian employee is reminded that he has definite responsibilities towards an employer, whether he be a Christian or not. (I Timothy 6:1; Titus 2:9). Similarly, employers are told to treat their employees justly and fairly, knowing that they themselves are answerable to their Heavenly Master. (Colossians 4:1). They are to recognise that "the labourer deserves his wages". (Luke 10:7; I Timothy 5:18).

New Testament ethics do not, however, provide us with a blueprint for a just society. Had our Lord provided such an ideal His teaching would have been as limited to His age and environment as Islam is so largely to the Arabia of Mahomet's time. The Christian ethic cannot be separated from Christian doctrine, and used as a panacea for the troubles of a world as yet unevangelised. At the same time, we must not be content to regard Christianity as relevant only to individual spiritual needs, and as having nothing to say, whether in judgment or in hope, concerning the social order in which men live. When Philemon received back his runaway slave as a "brother beloved", the difference of social status became far less important than the bond which united them in Christian love. Relationships were transformed although the social order remained unchanged.

From a Christian standpoint, if an industrial system is to function properly effort must be devoted to useful ends. The interests of the consumer should be rated higher than those of the manufacturer or distributor, and a fair policy of wages and work is incumbent on both employer and employee. It is a proper Christian concern that the natural resources of a country should be put to the best possible use. No Christian can be happy if relatively useless industries flourish while essential trades languish. A Christian cannot acquiesce in a situation where the heaping up of a large personal fortune is the main objective, or where employees are treated as mere machines. On the other hand it is equally repugnant to Christians when workers use their collective bargaining power for purely selfish ends.

A number of issues arise in modern industry which call for consideration—one of these is competition. There is a trend today towards more competitive industry. The simple theory of price competition is that the man who can make a product cheaper than the next man is entitled to sell it cheaper, and thereby gain a larger share of the market. This helps to keep down the cost of goods, and is in the public interest in stimulating the growth of the more efficient firms. Any competition which produces improved methods or improved products is praiseworthy. In practice, however, the situation is almost always more complicated than this. For the Christian, his guiding rule must be that he should treat others with the respect that he would like to receive from them. In a competitive world, he too must be competitive, but he must not earn the reputation of screwing the last ounce out of every transaction. His concern for the truth must also be paramount. This should be seen in the claims made for a particular product, as well as in the assessing of delivery dates. The salesman who has Christian standards sets himself limits. It is the Christian's absolute obligation not to tell lies. This includes both what is said and what is implied.

Expense accounts is another area in which Christian witness is called for. The Christian should obviously not put down as "expenses" costs incurred while entertaining friends. The Christian salesman should be particularly careful to decide the exact level of entertainment appropriate to a particular customer. A Christian must be concerned to avoid anything which savours of bribery. The Bible clearly condemns the giving of gifts to judges, and, although bribing a magistrate or judge is more serious than bribing a man who has to decide between different tenders, the principle is similar. Payment to pervert judgment is always wrong, whatever its scale, and a Christian will want nothing to do with it.

Advertising is another topic calling for consideration. The Christian who has any say in the advertising policy of his firm would want to avoid advertisements which are undisguised appeals to covetousness or based on eroticism. Vance Packard in *The Hidden Persuaders* illustrates the dangers of a lack of respect for human personality in advertising. The Christian is likely to be at a disadvantage where he is faced by competitors' claims which he does not think it right to match. The Christian must remember that his customer is a man created by God as a rational being and must be respected as such. In the world of advertising great emphasis is placed upon the "techniques of persuasion", covering such matters as the use of catch phrases and sales psychology. Advertisements are so designed as to appeal to our underlying semi-conscious or unconscious motives. The advertiser tends to exploit human weaknesses, and, in these days in particular, the appeal is often made to the erotic and acquisitive elements in man. In this area, the Christian objective should be to influence advertising methods and raise the general standard. Many Christians would feel, with considerable justification, that a great deal of modern advertising lies counter to the whole spirit of Christianity, and bases its appeal on man's lower nature.

It is hardly surprising that in the modern "rat race" which characterises our Western society, there are those who are tempted to opt out altogether. Whereas it is the divine intention that daily work should be satisfying, there are an increasing number of people who feel that real life only begins after the day's work is done. Grievous, however, as the situation may be we have to come to terms with society, and seek to apply our Christian principles, however difficult that may be.

The debate to-day in industry largely concerns the relative merits of different economic systems. Socialism or Capitalism? Are we for or against nationalisation? Under purely socialistic economics, resources are centrally owned and centrally co-ordinated. Under pure capitalistic economics ownership and co-ordination are decentralised. In fact, under modern socialist economics, while ownership is to some extent centralised, large areas of co-ordination remain de-centralised, whereas most capitalists are now moving towards the idea that some central planning has its place in the economic system. As far as a Christian is concerned, he is guided particularly by the two basic principles—that man was made in the image of God and is personally accountable to Him for all his acts, and that man has a responsibility to his fellows, and is to love both God and his neighbour.

The Christian above all respects the dignity of the individual. This brings him to have compassion on his fellows and not to despise them. He knows the power of God to change the most debased man or woman into a saint. He understands that he must love even his enemies. To the Christian, no one is "beyond the pale". No man, however degraded and however hostile, can be dismissed as of no account. The duty of compassion and care for our brother and our neighbour is taught from beginning to end of the Bible. Since the Christian is concerned for the freedom and the good of others, he will be reluctant to see too much concentration of power in any one quarter, including economic power. Essential economic freedom means that a man should have the right to change his job. He must have an income in cash rather than in kind; he must also have ready access to essential goods and services. An increased national standard of living may rightly be regarded as a proper Christian objective, but not as an end in itself. While the Christian will not want to overturn existing property rights, he will be anxious to see that property is acquired in a fair and rational way and that there is no aggregation of private wealth which would result in undue concentration of economic power.

The New Testament is full of injunctions to care for "the widow and fatherless". The Christian will be particularly concerned to ensure that some provision is made for those unable to earn their own living. Many Christians would feel that the compromise between socialism and capitalism found in Britain and elsewhere has much to commend it.

Christians maintain that conditions of work must be such as recognise the true value of human personality. Although factory working conditions have improved immeasurably, the growth of mechanisation has meant the worker is becoming increasingly depersonalised. The Christian should be concerned to see men are given the opportunity to exercise, within their powers, both initiative and responsibility, although this becomes increasingly difficult with the advance of automation.

We must now look at the question of Trade Unionism. A Trade Union has been defined as "the means by which the interests of the worker as a person can be pressed against the management with a force equivalent to that which the management itself can deploy". From time to time we read that a Christian has refused, on conscientious grounds, to join a Union and that pressure has been put on his employer to dismiss him. The argument against joining a Union is usually based on the injunction, "Do not be mismated with unbelievers". (II Cor. 6:14). It is hard to accept this interpretation of the "unequal yoke" in the light of the general tenor of New Testament teaching, especially passages such as Romans chapter 13. The "unequal yoke" surely refers to a much more intimate relationship, such as marriage. The question that we ask is—"Is a Trade Union in itself an association worthy of a Christian's support and membership?" It is worth noting that those companies with the strongest Christian tradition often have also the strongest Trade Union tradition. The Christian faith teaches respect for the individual, therefore if society respects the individual he must be protected from the possibility of exploitation by those who employ him. It is true that if all employers lived up to Christian ideals, there would be no need for Unions. In the world as it is, however, the trade union provides negotiating machinery for the wage-earner. Christians should not simply accept unions grudgingly as a necessary evil. Since the Christian supports an order of society, he should therefore support those bodies which are concerned with resolving men's disputes with one another in an orderly way.

Frank Deeks, a Christian shop steward, in his paperback *Shop-floor Christianity* quotes the well-known words of Burke—"All that is needed for evil to succeed is for good men to do nothing" and illustrates the point in the following way: "All Trade Union officers are elected by the membership, but only by that part of the membership that bothers to vote. In fact, this is just a tiny minority. Consider: there is not one Communist Member of Parliament, yet a lot of Communists are in

Trade Union leadership. Why? Because Trade Union leaders are usually elected by 0.5% or less of the membership, while the General Election turnout is between 60% and 80%."

The right to form Trade Unions and the right to withhold labour normally go together, because the right to withhold labour is usually the only sanction available to "the working man". Strikes do, of course, dramatically draw attention to a particular grievance. A long history of industrial unrest suggests deep-rooted problems such as a long-term decline of the industry, a history of insecurity of employment, or a prolonged period of bad management and labour relations. At the present time the major problem of industry, and of good government, is how to combine the legitimate workings of industrial bargaining with a reasonably high degree of employment, and increasing inflation.

To reduce the number of strikes there needs to be a raising of the standard of personnel management. It has been said that a strike is usually, if not always, a symptom of pathological labour relations.

It has sometimes been pointed out that it is not easy for professional people who negotiate their own terms of work, and whose jobs demand individual judgment and initiative, to see the need for the worker to accept collective discipline. Recognition and the ability to enforce agreements are the twin pillars on which a Union stands, and without which it cannot function. The so-called "closed shop" is the Union's sanction against its own members, just as the strike is its sanction against the employer. Strike action is particularly repugnant to the Christian, because he recognises he is putting the general public to inconvenience and hardship, in order to enforce his own sectional interests. The Christian regards patience as a virtue and he should never be exasperated or stampeded into ill-considered action. He should try all other means before allowing a trial of strength and should always do his best to promote the rational settlement of disputes.

On the matter of strikes we will leave the last word to Frank Deeks—"The only possible bargaining power he has is the withdrawal of his work or the threat to do so. He has no other weapon. Like all weapons it should be used only when all else fails...Likewise, when a company feels its employees are going beyond reasonable action, it must have the right to say, Enough! We withhold your work."

It is the duty of the Christian to support every movement which helps towards better working conditions and to submit to every wise rule which has been proved to be for the benefit of the community. The Christian is under obligation to recognise the social order in which he finds himself until that order is changed for a better one by constitutional means. It must be admitted, however, that sometimes the tacit acquiescence of Christians in the status quo has made Christianity appear to some as irrelevant to the needs of modern man. When the comforts of religion are offered as a substitute for the bare necessities of earthly life, not only is religion discredited, but the suspicion is created that the promise of blessings beyond the grave is merely an evasion of the demands for justice in this present life.

It is sometimes claimed that Calvin's "asceticism within the world" did much to prepare the way for modern capitalism, but in fairness to Calvin he did much to prevent merchants in Geneva selling goods at unjust prices and insisted on a reasonable interest rate on loans. Likewise, the Puritans stressed the principle of stewardship in the use of wealth, although the later Puritans did tend to regard prosperity as a sign that they were among the elect. To this extent they paved the way for what Tawney calls "the triumph of the economic virtues".

As we have already stated, New Testament ethics do

not provide us with a blue-print for a just society, but neither do they permit us to be indifferent to the needs of others or allow us to acquiesce in injustices. As far as party politics is concerned, there is much truth in the dictum—"It is better for the Christian faith itself if it is not identified with one party, but carries its spirit into all". One thing can be said which has no political overtones—Christians can never be happy about a situation in which human interests are over-ridden by commercial interests. People, to a Christian, always matter more than things.

## 12. WEALTH AND POVERTY

There is an old saying to the effect that one half of the world does not know how the other half lives. Even in our Western society there are strange anomalies. Basically we live in an affluent age, yet side by side with wealth there is dire poverty and need. According to figures given by Dr. William Barclay in *Ethics in a Permissive Society*, in spite of the affluent society there were in Britain in 1965/6 1,500,000 households with no indoor lavatory, 3,640,000 without a fixed inside bath, 3,000,000 with no hot water tap and 246,000 without even a cold tap. On average two thousand people "sleep rough" in London every night. If we took a look at the "third world" we should find an even greater disparity of conditions. The developed countries are now on average 12 times richer than the poorer nations and the gap is widening.

The New Testament speaks out against the pursuit of riches in themselves even more strongly than the Old Testament. In the Old Testament material prosperity was often interpreted as the sign of divine favour (Psalm 1:3; Prov. 3:16, 8:18, 10:22, 30:8–9 etc.), although the prophets did not fail to expose the sins to which the rich are peculiarly prone. Apart from the Epistle of James the New Testament says comparatively little about the evils of oppression and exploitation as such. In the New Testament the primary evil is seen not so much in the possession of riches, but in the sin of avarice which so easily besets the rich man. Material wealth is pictured as something to be given away in order that a man may secure true spiritual riches (Luke 6:38; 12:33,34). Our Lord's whole emphasis was on the fact that material possessions are quite secondary in importance (Luke 12:15; cf. Romans 14:17). There is a constant danger of earthly things taking the place of heavenly things in the rich man's affections.

There is divine authority for getting, owning and using money (Deut. 8:18; Eccl. 5:19). Paul gives Timothy instructions as to the way money should be used (I Timothy 6:17–19). It is noteworthy that trading and investing are referred to in acceptable terms in the Bible. Slaves are warned against purloining (Titus 2:10). It is taken for granted that the man who plants a vineyard will eat the fruit of it (I Corinthians 9:7). It is assumed that men have a right to determine what they shall do with what belongs to them (Matthew 20:15; Acts 5:4).

"Affluence in the hands of fallen man is a double-edged blessing and the source of much evil" (R. H. Fuller and B. K. Rice: *Christianity and the Affluent Society*). It is sometimes said that prosperity is the blessing of the Old Testament and adversity of the New Testament. Bishop Gore has stated "there is more in the Gospels against being rich and in favour of being poor than most of us like to recognise". Luke in particular records a number of sayings of our Lord that appear to militate against the possessions of wealth, and to extol the virtues of poverty (cf. Luke 1:53; 3:11; 4:18; 6:24 ff.; 12:13–21; 14:12–14; 16:19–31). The incident of the rich young ruler is recorded in all three Synoptic Gospels (Matthew 19:16–26; Mark 10:17–26; Luke 18:18–26). Centuries before similar warnings had been given in the Old Testament (Deut. 8:11–14; Eccl. 5:13,14,17). In the Old Testament the poor man is represented as being under God's special care (Psalm 9:18; 68:10; 72:12; 69:33; 109:31; 140:12).

Our Lord does not teach that material things are in themselves evil. Such parables as those of the talents and the pounds suggest that He did not disapprove of the possession of wealth, but was concerned to stress its right use. Dives was not condemned because he was rich, but because he failed to use his riches rightly. The Centurion on the other hand who built the synagogue was praised for so doing (Luke 7:1–10). The disciples themselves owned fishing boats and nets and returned to them after the crucifixion (John 21:3). The home to which Jesus Himself often resorted at Bethany was clearly relatively well-to-do (John 12:3). The New Testament assumes the Christian will earn his living like the rest and meet his obligations (cf. I Corinthians 4:12; I Thess. 2:9; 2 Thess. 3:7–8; Acts 20:34). Money is something which may be put to good use. It may be used to make friends. "Use the destructible wealth to purchase the eternal wealth of human friendships" urged our Lord (Luke 16:9). The Samaritan put his money to good use—to meet human need (Luke 10:30–37). Similarly, money can provide hospitality for the unfortunate (Luke 14:12–14). The possession of money makes alms-giving possible, although even this can be robbed of any spiritual value if it is done from wrong motives (Matthew 6:1–4). Money may be legitimately used to express gratitude and love, but should not be wasted (Matthew 26:6–13).

Our Lord did, however, point out that it was a sheer miracle for a rich man to be saved (Matthew 19:23–26; Mark 10:23–25; Luke 18:24–25). Wealth tends to drug the higher sensitivities of the soul (Matthew 13:22). The heart tends to go with the treasure (Matthew 6:19–34). Covetousness petrifies the heart and darkens the inner eye (Matthew 6:22). Wealth tends to give man an illusory sense of security and satisfaction. When our Lord said,

"Lay not up for yourselves treasure upon earth", He was not saying that the Christian must not save or invest money, but that he must have a responsible attitude towards its use. The really worthwhile things in life are such that money cannot buy (Mark 8:36).

Supremely money is regarded as an instrument in the hands of men. Of itself it is neutral, being neither good nor evil. It does, however, act as the mirror of our inner nature. Like time and talents it can be used to the enrichment of a man's character, to the welfare of his fellow men, and above all to the glory of God. It is a question of having the right priorities and being alive to the inherent dangers which riches bring in their train (I Timothy 6:5,6, 9,10).

Bishop Ryle made some helpful comments concerning the use and abuse of wealth: "For money Achan brought defeat on the armies of Israel and death on himself. For money, Balaam sinned against light and tried to curse God's people. For money, Delilah betrayed Samson to the Philistines. For money, Gehazi lied to Naaman and Elisha. For money, Ananias and Sapphira became the first hypocrites in the early Church and lost their lives. For money, Judas Iscariot sold Christ and was ruined eternally." The Bishop went on to point out that two thirds of all the strikes, quarrels and law-suits in the world arise from one single cause—money. He summed up the situation in these words: "Money is one of the most unsatisfying of all possessions. It takes away some cares, no doubt, but it brings with it quite as many cares as it takes away. There is the trouble in the getting of it. There is anxiety in the keeping of it. There are temptations in the use of it. There is guilt in the abuse of it. There is sorrow in the losing of it. There is perplexity in the disposing of it."

While the Scriptures abound in warnings against a wrong attitude to wealth, we do find every encouragement to give. In Old Testament and New Testament alike promises are held out to those who give willingly and generously (Deut. 15:10; Psalm 41:1; Proverbs 3:9; Malachi 3:10,11; Luke 6:38; Acts 10:2–4; 20:35). God's people in the Old Testament were taught to tithe (Genesis 14:18–20; 28:20,21,22b; Leviticus 27:30; Matthew 23:23). Our Lord stressed the need for unostentatious giving (Matthew 6:2–4) and showed that the value of the gift lies in what is retained rather than the actual amount given (Mark 12:41–44). The apostle Paul taught that giving should be related to income, and should be systematic (I Cor. 16:1). The inspiration for Christian giving is to be found in God's own self-giving (II Corinthians 8:9). The New Testament records many instances of generous giving (Acts 9:39; 11:27–30; Romans 15:26).

We conclude then that at best wealth is a secondary good—it is good to have neither too much nor too little (Proverbs 30:8 and 9). Wealth is no substitute for character and goodness; worldly riches are at best perishable (Prov. 27:24; Matt. 6:19–21; Luke 12:13–21). The love of money is at the root of every evil (I Tim.6:10). Those in positions of leadership in the Church must be free from avarice (I Tim. 3:2,8; Titus 1:7; I Peter5:2). A man's true character is seen in his handling of money matters (Luke 16:10–12). The more money a man has the more temptations he has. Wealth is not so much an evil to be shunned, as a gift to be shared (I Tim. 6:17ff.).

We could scarcely do better than take a leaf out of John Wesley's book. When up at Oxford his yearly income was £30, £2 of which he gave away. As the years passed his income rose even as high as £120 a year, but he contrived to live on £28 and to give the rest away. His maxim was, "Save all you can so that you may give all you can." It is to be regretted that the giving of Christians does not always keep pace with their growing affluence. The Christian is bound to see wealth in terms of stewardship. Greater riches bring greater responsibilities. Having said this we should add that there are times when the mere giving of money is not enough. As William Barclay points out: "To give money may be at times an evasion of a still greater responsibility...there are times when the giving of oneself is the greatest gift of all."

## 13. GAMBLING AND RELATED ISSUES

Gambling may be defined as the redistribution of wealth by the exploitation of risk, to the loss of one party and the gain of another. Canon Peter Green gives this definition: "A gamble is a transaction between two parties whereby the transfer of something of value from one to the other is made dependent upon chance in such a way that the whole gain of one party equals the whole loss of the other." In a word, gambling is an attempt to gain something for nothing. The gain of the winner is at the expense of the loser. Success in gambling depends entirely on the failure of others. It is an attempt to batten on one's fellow men. While it may be permissible to harness chance for amusement in a simple game, it is another matter to harness chance to a contract whereby money or goods of value are exchanged on the basis of chance.

In the main, three forms of gambling have been the subject of legislation in Britain, and were named in the title of the Betting, Gaming and Lotteries Act 1963. Betting is the laying of stakes on the result of an event whose outcome is unknown. Football pools are a form of betting. Gaming is the laying of stakes on a game of pure chance or in a game where skill and chance are found together. Bingo has some of the characteristics of both gaming and a lottery. Lotteries depend on a draw in which chances are sold at an equal price, and the prizes derive from the money staked by the purchase of tickets. Sweepstakes and raffles are the commonest form of lottery, apart from the Premium Bond draw in which the interest on the nominal value of the bonds is staked for the chance of a prize.

The law controls football pools through the local authority, bookmakers by justices' permit, and betting offices by licences which are renewable annually, and to the issue and renewal of which objections may be made. Lotteries are subject to stringent conditions, e.g. they may not be used for private gain, and no person under 16 years of age may buy or sell tickets for a lottery. All gaming is now legalised, but loop-holes in the 1960 Act have made it possible for the establishment of bingo and gaming clubs, many of which have become centres of socially undesirable and harmful activities.

Objections to gambling may be raised on several counts—for one thing it is a misuse of money. In the last analysis there are only three honest ways of getting money—by working for it, selling something for it, or receiving it as a gift. In gambling there is no exchange of goods or services. In a commendable economic transaction both parties gain, but not so in a gamble. The whole idea of gambling is directly opposed to the Christian view of life. Christ pictured life as being the object of the providential care of a loving Father, not the product of blind chance. Gambling is a virtual denial of faith in God and an ordered universe. Furthermore, gambling panders to human weakness. It encourages the spirit of covetousness, the inordinate desire to have more than one's fair share of the good things of life with the minimum of personal effort. Our Lord taught that it was more blessed to give than to receive. There can be no common ground between this and the gambling spirit which looks for as much as possible in return for as little as possible. Gambling, therefore, cuts right across the principles of Christian stewardship. It inevitably leads to the corruption of character. Character deteriorates when "something for nothing" is the chief aim, and all forms of gambling tend to attract weak and vicious people. It encourages personal dishonesty and absenteeism in industry. Lazy people grow lazier whilst waiting for their luck to turn. Gambling also militates against home and family life. More often than not the betting man is handling money which rightly belongs to his family. Poverty is unnecessarily created by irresponsible gambling and human suffering is the consequence. Also, it can so easily become an addiction. The problem of the compulsive gambler is very much with us, and all too often it is allied to crime, as the loser in his desperation seeks to make good his losses. Gambling has become a major social problem, and is also a colossal waste of the nation's resources. It is conservatively estimated that in any one year the turnover on horse and greyhound racing in Britain is at least £1,200,000,000. The annual turnover on bingo clubs in the United Kingdom is probably between £30,000,000 and £40,000,000. About 12,000,000 people regularly do football pools and there are 15/16,000 betting shops in Britain. Gambling is a symptom of a sickness in our society.

It is often argued that Premium Bonds are a form of gambling and there is some truth in this although the gamble here is on the interest not on the capital.

There is an increasing pressure in various quarters in Britain to have a national lottery, and it is argued that, since gambling flourishes, it should be made to serve useful purposes. But there are serious arguments against such a lottery. The lottery tends towards an uncritical use of money. By implication it means that medical facilities, scientific research, adequate sports facilities, and similar desirable objectives are regarded either as subjects for charity or as optional extras only to be achieved by the lottery. These matters are of community responsibility, and provision for them should be rationally determined.

We would not dream of financing national defence in any such way. The lottery is also a costly and wasteful method of raising money. At least as much money is needed for prizes and expenses as may be set apart for the object in view. The lottery tends to exploit the need of the poorer members of society: in spite of their financial need, and in the shadowy hope of removing it, they buy lottery tickets. The lottery tends to take advantage of those who are least capable of affording it or of assessing the chances of winning. Important public work should be rationally and seriously financed and undertaken. It cannot be the mark of a mature and responsible society that it should lean unnecessarily on gathering and distributing wealth by chance. The use of a lottery indicates over-sophistication rather than maturity.

It is sometimes claimed that insurance is a form of gambling, but this is not the case. Insurance is the reverse of gambling, and can only be wise in so far as gambling is foolish. Insurance represents a co-operative and mutually beneficial transaction, while gambling is a competitive and anti-social practice. By means of insurance the inevitable risks of life are spread over as large a company of persons as possible. It may be regarded as a way of bearing one another's burdens, and "so fulfilling the law of Christ". The object of a gamble is to exploit chance and concentrate the advantage of exceptional luck on a single person. The object of insurance is to eliminate as far as possible the element of chance, and spread the advantage or disadvantage over as many people as possible. Insurance introduces the law of averages to eliminate chance, while gambling puts unnecessary risk in the place of ultimate control.

It is often argued that the transactions which take place on the Stock Exchange are a form of gambling. It must be admitted that there are some transactions which do come into this category, but it would be quite wrong to suggest that all business transactions on the

Stock Exchange are a form of gambling. In a capitalistic society it is necessary to have a Stock Exchange in order to handle the buying and selling of securities. There may be speculation on the Stock Exchange which is tantamount to gambling, as for example, when a holding with very high risk is purchased without adequate rational grounds, or when an attempt is made to profit from the rapidly changing prices of stocks and shares. Rightly understood, however, the Stock Exchange provides an argument against gambling, and emphasises the importance of dealing as carefully and rationally as possible with the risks which cannot be avoided in all financial transactions. One of the main functions of the Stock Exchange is the assessment of the economic worth of one investment as against another. It combines the need of industry for long-term investment with the desire of the investor to have ready access to his capital should he need it. Gambling on the Stock Exchange must be distinguished from investment for a capital gain over a reasonable period, which very often amounts to merely the measure of inflation during the period of ownership. One of the evils of inflation is that the fall in the value of money discourages saving.

In industry both capital and labour are required. Since both are needed for production both have a right to share in the fruits of production. So long as the right of property ownership is conceded it is impossible logically to deny the right to interest on invested capital. Furthermore, there is no legitimate reason why anyone who has money to invest should not seek out the investments most likely to pay good dividends. The rate of interest is the price paid for the use of money over a period. The case is different, however, with the man who invests his money not with the intention of contributing a necessary factor—i.e., capital for the production of wealth—but merely with the intention of selling his shares again at the earliest possible opportunity and realising a quick profit. Such a man contributes nothing to industry but merely skims the profits of other men's labours. This is speculative dealing in stocks and shares —buying for the rise and selling for the fall—without any intention of holding them as an investment. Parables such as those of the talents and the pounds do suggest that there is nothing intrinsically wrong in seeking interest on capital. An individual may invest his money in stocks and shares directly or he may leave it to others to invest on his behalf by allowing it to accumulate in a Deposit Account or by buying units of a Unit Trust. Christians may have qualms about investing in certain Unit Trusts on the grounds that they may be contributing through such trusts to doubtful enterprises. Obviously, due thought should be given to this question, and every attempt made to restrict oneself to investments which do not arouse conscientious scruples.

Archbishop William Temple stated that the judgement of any action depended on three things—"the character expressed in the act, the principle involved, and the consequences resulting." It is mainly on these three counts that gambling stands condemned. Obviously not all forms of gambling have the same moral, social and economic significance. The fact is, however, that gambling in general gives rise to a range of personal and social problems, and the Christian Church is bound to set its face against anything which can destroy a man or society. Since the legislation of 1963, whereby Parliament made gambling legal and enabled betting shops to do business openly, there has been considerable increase in gambling. Casino-type gambling is a growing industry, the profitability of which is indicated by the massive licence fees paid by promoters. It should be a matter of general concern that such a high proportion of the population should be caught up in what is at its least an uncreative pastime and at its worst an industry geared to the exploitation of human weakness.

If the Church is ready to recognise gambling as a major social evil it should endeavour to see that its own hands are clean, even to the extent of ensuring that such "harmless" things as raffles are excluded.

## 14. THE CHRISTIAN AND THE STATE

The State, like the family, is a divinely ordained institution, put there for the restraint of evil and the promotion of the common good of society. To live in a community and to enjoy all its amenities, and to avoid the responsibilities of citizenship, is definitely wrong and inevitably produces evil results. Christians are members of the Church, and yet they have to recognise the authority of the State. Even a godless State demands recognition, since by its very constitution it does to a certain extent fulfil the divine purpose. In so far as the State contravenes the law of God in certain respects, it stands condemned, but in so far as it serves the economy of God as a whole, it calls for acceptance.

Our Lord lived at a time when His countrymen were subject to Roman rule. Had He been willing to become their political Messiah, many would no doubt have rallied to His support. But in fact, He very largely ignored the political issues of His time. When the Pharisees came with their loaded question—"Is it lawful to pay taxes to Caesar or not?" He called for a silver denarius on which were inscribed Caesar's name and image, and told them to "Render to Caesar the things that are Caesar's, and to God the things which are God's". (Matthew 22:15–22). He recognised the legitimate claims of government alongside man's obligation toward God. By His example our Lord taught submissiveness towards the civil authorities (Matthew 17:27), but made it clear that worship is for God alone (Matthew 4:10). He consistently refused to identify His Kingdom with the political State. He knew, as He told Pilate at His trial, that His Kingdom was not of this world and could not be achieved along the lines of the nations of this world. (John 18:33–38).

The Apostle Paul saw the State as an institution appointed by God, perhaps not in the original plan of creation, but certainly to meet the needs of a fallen world as an instrument of God's wrath. The order maintained by governments is in some measure an expression of God's own order. A king or government does not obtain power either from purely natural causes or from a social contract, but from God (Romans 13:1–7). Christians are exhorted to pray for the civil authorities. (I Tim. 2:1–2). The "powers that be" are ordained to discourage social evil and to encourage social good—to create and maintain good order.

Christian freedom is not to be made an excuse for failing to meet moral obligations imposed by the State. (I Peter 2:16f). As citizens we should be submissive to governmental authority, and should pay all that is due to the civil powers, both in taxes and in respect and honour. Troeltach comments: "Paul did not merely recognise the State as permitted by God, but prized it as an institution which at least cared for justice, order and morality". The "powers that be" serve to check wrong-doing, and to resist a magistrate may be to resist God. (Romans 13:2). Even a bad government is a lesser evil than no government at all. Paul credits the Roman government with being a restraining influence as far as anti-Christ is concerned. (II Thessalonians 2:vv. 5,7,8). At the same time, it should be pointed out that Paul discouraged the use by Christians of heathen law courts in matters at issue between themselves

(I Corinthians 6). Peter argued along similar lines. (I Peter 2:13–17).

In the Old Testament there was no clear division between religion and government, since the Hebrew nation was ideally a theocracy. Civil laws carried, therefore, a divine sanction. Christianity brought about an entirely new state of affairs. Christians were not to be identified with any one nation, but constituted a recognisable group within different nations. The New Testament never thinks of the Christian as primarily a citizen of an earthly State. He "is the citizen of another kingdom, and it is thence that he derives his way of thinking, judging and feeling. . . He may be in the world, it is true, but all his ties are elsewhere." The Christian's citizenship is in heaven, yet he does still have responsibilities on earth. (Phil. 3:20).

In a democracy—government of the people by the people for the people—it would seem that the command to render unto Caesar implies participation to some degree in the processes of government and law-making. Christians should be concerned to promote the best interests of society, even though it would be unreasonable to expect to impose the full Christian ethic on a mixed society. The Christian's duty to an earthly State will vary according to circumstances. It is possible for a government to abdicate its God-given duties to such an extent and to prove so utterly evil that Christian men may feel that they are absolved from their duty of obedience, and are justified in seeking its downfall and replacement. The Christian cannot, of course, obey commands which are in direct conflict with specific Christian teaching.

T. M. Taylor in *The Heritage of the Reformation* states "The obedience which the Christian man owes to the State is never absolute, but at the most partial and contingent. It follows that the Christian lives always in a tension between two competing claims: that in certain circumstances disobedience to the command of the State may be not only a right but also a duty. This has been classical Christian doctrine ever since the Apostles declared that they ought to obey God rather than men".

Augustine, and later Pope Gelasius I, developed the doctrine of two kingdoms—the Kingdom of God concerned with spiritual interests, and the kingdom of the world concerned with temporal interests such as the maintenance of law and order. Each kingdom holds sway over its own sphere, but they should work together for the common good. As the power of the Church grew it claimed supremacy over the State, with the right not merely to consecrate kings and emperors, but also to depose them. In 1302 Pope Boniface VIII issued a Bull declaring that the temporal sword was under his control.

Luther also followed this teaching regarding the two kingdoms, and claimed that the secular power must not interfere in matters of faith; but he accepted the divine authority of the civil powers and the Christian duty of obedience. Calvin went somewhat further, and regarded the civil power as being responsible under God for preserving true religion. Calvin thought of Church and State as being ideally united in one object—the promotion of an ordered society, a Christian commonwealth, in which the will of God is done on earth.

In England there was at the Reformation a widespread concern to preserve for the State a Christian policy, and this led to the concept of a national church intended to blend secular and religious interests for the spiritual, political and economic good of the community. Thus all citizens of the national State were, broadly speaking, regarded as members of the national church, and the secular community was committed to a Christian ideology. The Independents took a different line, and contended that the Church was a brotherhood of individuals called out from society to form a new community.

The question arises whether and in what circumstances the church should take political action. In the early 19th century the Clapham Sect took such action, forming themselves into a kind of Christian pressure group. There are, however, good reasons against the Church as such entering party politics. Inevitably there is a degree of compromise in much legislation, and it is inconsistent for the Church as such to be a party to this. Many issues are not sufficiently clear-cut for the Church to speak unitedly. Furthermore, active political involvement may give the impression that the Church's main interest is in secular affairs. As Professor J. N. D. Anderson points out, however, "Christians have both the right and the duty to try to convince their fellow citizens, whatever their religious or ideological affiliation, of the relevance and importance of those principles which they believe to be essential to the well-being of society and of its individual members." It follows that Christians should do what they can to influence public opinion and to support all worthy beneficial initiatives. The Christian is bound to maintain the existence of transcendental justice and the basic standard of right and wrong which is independent of the vagaries of contemporary evil.

The Church should "speak a discerning word to each concrete situation". To quote Archbishop Temple: "The Church must announce Christian principles, and point out where the existing social order is in conflict with them. It must then pass on to Christian citizens, acting in their civil capacity, the task of reshaping the existing order in closer conformity to the principles."

Christians are bound to challenge any view of the State which reduces the individual to the status of a mere cog in a machine, or which debases his dignity as a rational and moral being created in the image of God. The Christian sees the State primarily as ordained by God to serve the best interests of its individual citizens.

The notion that the perfectionist ethic of Christian

love can be applied directly to any and every imaginable social order corrupted by sin falls very far short of Christian realism. As we have already observed there is no suggestion in the New Testament that the Christian ethic may be separated from Christian doctrine and used as a panacea for the problems of a world as yet unevangelised. Paul's teaching on slavery is an imperishable witness to the possibility of living the Christian life in a social order fundamentally opposed to the Christian estimate of man. While social reform and the message of the gospel may be intimately related, they nevertheless belong to different spheres. At the same time, men with the spirit of love in their hearts will naturally be interested in everything that will benefit their fellow men, and in this sense it may be said that Christian ethical teaching is on the side of reform.

The content of Christian moral judgments and the specific forms of Christian action will differ in differing social contexts. The main task of our Lord, however, was not the establishment of an improved economic or political system, but the founding of a fellowship to express in its conduct those qualities of righteousness, love and truth which preserve and ennoble human society.

The Christian will always seek to exert his influence upon society by non-forceful means. The question arises, however, at what point, if at all, should tyranny be resisted? What means, if any, may be taken to get an unjust law changed or a tyrannical government overthrown? What if constitutional methods prove ineffective? Is there such a thing as a "Just Revolution" —a revolution in which even convinced Christians may, with good conscience, participate? Is the obligation of obedience to the "powers that be" (cf. Rom. 13:1–7; I Peter 2:13–17) applicable whatever the circumstances?

The first essential for a "Just Revolution" must be a "just cause", and this implies that every constitutional method of effecting social change has been tried without success. Another criterion is the means used and the extent of the suffering which is likely to follow. The weight of human suffering involved in armed rebellion must be balanced against the suffering involved in continued tyranny. Civil violence may have such tragic consequences that a Christian may well think that it cannot be proportionate to the good which may be achieved. Violence tends to create violence. Many revolutions have overturned one régime only to establish another, no less unjust and tyrannical than the one replaced.

In the book *Is Revolution Change?* Rene Padilla states the Christian's position in these terms: "The Christian agrees with the revolutionary in his dissatisfaction with the state of things as they are, and the desire for a change in the situation... He disagrees with the revolutionary, nevertheless, in that he does not believe in violence as *the* solution for social problems, *the* road that leads to the perfect society. ...there may be occasions when the balance of power, necessary for justice, demands violence as the comparatively lesser evil... What simply does not fit into the mental system of the Christian is violence as the norm of history." When our Lord was on earth He took an uncompromising stand against oppression, but so did He against those who wanted to take the law into their own hands, and change the situation by means of force.

Christian history provides us with strangely divergent reactions to revolution. We have Luther's attitude to the Peasants' Revolt in 1524–5. In the eyes of the Reformer, the peasants in revolting had clearly broken Christ's command to render to Caesar the things that are Caesar's, and, therefore, they stood condemned. Luther went out of his way to encourage his followers to deal summarily with the rebels, "remembering that nothing can be more poisonous, hurtful, or devilish than a rebel." We have now turned full circle to the extent that we find the World Council of Churches voting sums of money to encourage insurrection against racism in South Africa. What shall we say to these things? Clearly, Christians must be alive to political issues. They must become involved in the community. They must be prepared to use every conceivable constitutional means to redress wrong and injustice, but involvement in armed insurrection hardly seems to fit into the picture. Living in two worlds at the same time inevitably raises problems. To seek the cloister may be the answer for some, but not for most. For the ordinary Christian involvement and detachment must go hand in hand. The Christian recognises both Christ and Caesar, but he can never say: "Caesar is Lord". There are limits beyond which he cannot go. His ultimate loyalty is to Christ alone.

## 15. CHRISTIANITY AND DEMOCRACY

It is a mistake to think that Christianity and democracy are necessarily bound up together. Christians at various times and in various places have lived happily under despotic regimes although political tyranny has tended to bring the State into conflict with the Church since, all too often, the supreme authority of God and liberty of conscience have been denied. Generally, Christians tend to opt for some form of democracy of the constitutional type. It would be quite wrong, however, to identify the Christian faith in any legalistic manner with any of the established Western democratic structures.

Democracy often claims to be the greatest political achievement of modern Western civilisation, though it was discovered by the Ancient Greeks. Christianity has undoubtedly had a formative influence on the development of modern democracy, so much so that some have tended to regard it as simply the application of Christian ethics in the political sphere. There is, however, much in Western democracy which is opposed to Christian ethical and social ideals.

Democracy has often been defined as government *by* as well as *for* the people—in other words, the people have the final authority, and those who govern in their name are responsible to them. Democracy is government by consent in the sense that it is government by representatives who have the general approval of the majority. Democracy seeks to serve the common good of the community as a whole without bestowing advantages on any privileged group. It rejects the collectivistic theory that State, Class or Race transcend in importance the persons who are their members. Majority rule is the practical method adopted to secure the responsibility of representatives to the people and enable general policy to be determined by as large a proportion of the citizens as possible. In a truly democratic State free discussion is protected by the rights of free speech, a free press, and freedom of assembly.

Advocates of democracy would claim that government must be controlled by the people if their grievances are to be not merely heard but to be taken seriously. Lincoln said, "No man is good enough to govern another man without that other's consent."

Since man is a rational being he has a right to share in formulating the policies by which his society is to be governed. Democracy has always had faith in the dignity of man and in his creative possibilities. There is no evidence that a privileged class of any kind is politically wiser than the people as a whole. Democracy does imply, however, that there shall be a reasonably high standard of education available to all.

Democracy encourages independent thought and initiative rather than regimentation. The freedom of the individual is safeguarded. Democracy recognises the need for social change, but requires that such change shall be encompassed in an orderly manner. The fullest opportunity is afforded by a democracy for the exercise of social responsibility, and hence for the development of character.

Turning to the other side of the picture, democracy tends to encourage excessive individualism and self-interest. Some have seen democracy simply as a political system, the essence of which is universal suffrage and majority rule, with the result that each section of the community votes for its own interests and acts as a pressure group to influence legislation favourable to itself.

Democracy requires that the party in power shall not misuse their powers, and shall remain sensitive to the feelings and views of the electorate as a whole. Furthermore, the party in power shall not use their advantage unfairly to extend their term of office. Democracy has often been discredited when those holding office are such that they do not truly command the respect of the electorate.

Respect for the dignity and worth of each individual was lacking in the democratic "city-states" of ancient Greece. Slaves were excluded from the privileges of citizenship, and foreigners were regarded as "barbarians". In a democracy inspired by Christian ideals men cannot be depersonalised or treated merely as a means to an end. In a democracy worthy of the name there should be belief in a fundamental human equality which transcends all the actual inequalities. This conviction is a direct product of the Christian faith. Democracies have suffered from the subordination of duties to rights, and from pushing liberty to excess. The Biblical emphasis is upon concern for one's neighbour, and this makes liberty responsible.

A democracy that is based upon Christian realism about fallen human nature will be moderate in its expectations. It will be suspicious of absolute and final solutions of economic and social problems. To quote Niebuhr, it will be content to be "a method of finding proximate solutions for insoluble problems". A realistic view of man has helped men to see the necessity of imposing a limitation of power upon the representatives of the people. Democracy tacitly recognises that unbridled political power is dangerous and liable to abuse because of the corruption of human nature. Utopianism which overlooks universal human fallibility and sinfulness can tempt a revolutionary party to use the most ruthless means to attain its ends.

Christians are understandably suspicious of any political system which unduly exalts the state and submerges the individual citizen. The Bible stresses the infinite value of every human being in the sight of God, (Matt. 10. 10:29–31). Christians must challenge any view of the state which reduces the individual to the status of a mere cog in a gigantic machine, or which in any way debases the dignity, as a rational and moral being created in the image of God, of any man. The Christian sees the State primarily as ordained by God to serve the best interests of its individual citizens. The state should maintain and protect a strict and impartial justice for all its citizens—the law must be applicable to all without distinction. In so far as it is possible to do so, Christians should work to establish, to preserve or to improve existing political structures, and will want to bear in mind the fact that government should be based upon the consent and the participation of the people, and constitutional protection should be granted for the rights of minorities to organise politically and express their convictions.

A democracy by its very nature makes considerable demands upon the individual citizens of a country, and that would include Christians. Just as the voice of Christianity has often gone by default in the Trade Union movement, so Christian influence has not been exerted to anything like the extent it might have been in the country at large, because of apathy on the part of Christian electors. In a democratic country, rendering to Caesar the things which are Caesar's must include exercising one's franchise responsibly and taking an intelligent interest in the country's affairs.

We close with a quotation from Karl Barth, "It must

be admitted that the word and the concept 'democracy' (rule of the people) is powerless to describe even approximately the kind of State which, in the Christian view, most nearly corresponds to the divine ordinance. There is no reason, however, why it should be overlooked or denied that Christian choices and purposes in politics tend on the whole towards the form of State, which, if it is not actually realised in the so-called 'democracies', is at any rate more or less honestly intended and desired" (*Against the Stream*, p. 44).

# 16. CRIME AND PUNISHMENT

In his book *Crime in a Changing Society* H. Jones comments, "How a society treats its offenders is an index of its basic attitude towards human personality; if, for example, we ill-treat our thieves, we show only too clearly what we put first, property or people." Christians, bearing in mind the Biblical emphasis on the dignity of human personality, are bound to address themselves to the subject of crime and punishment.

At a time of mounting crime figures we need to ask whether there is anything in the structure of our modern society or in the dominant values by which it lives which accounts for the growth of criminal behaviour.

The present crime wave is one aspect of our rapidly changing society with its confusion of moral standards, and the weakening of social cohesion through the breakdown of traditional social patterns.

When assessing the place of punishment in our world —we find that in practice there is always a tension between our obligation to society and our obligation to the offender. A full assessment of responsibility is not within the ability of any Court or human being.

Professor Goodhart has said, "Retribution in punishment is an expression of the community's disapproval of crime, and if this retribution is not given recognition, then the disapproval may also disappear". Hitherto the core of punishment has been retribution—but modern thinking tends to suggest that the whole retributive notion is false.

Moberly in *The Ethics of Punishment* asks, "Should a criminal be regarded by society chiefly as a nuisance to be abated, an enemy to be crushed, a debtor to be made to pay, a patient to be treated or a refractory child to be disciplined?" In looking at the matter of punishment one must bear in mind all these aspects to some extent.

Apart from punishment in an ordered community law would rapidly cease to function. The right to impose law carries with it the right to enforce it. It would seem from a number of His parables that our Lord tacitly accepted the fact of imprisonment. Paul explicitly states that the magistrate "does not bear the sword in vain" (Rom. 13:4) which expresses justification of the State in exacting punishment. In civilised countries it is an accepted principle that in general the right to use force judicially is invested in civil authority. The State or a legally constituted authority within the State alone has the right to use force to secure the ends of justice. The question is whether this right is permissive in character, being warranted by the fact that the State has to deal with evil; or whether the right to use force is inherent in the State simply because it is the State. In considering this subject we need to view the question of punishment from several different angles.

When punishment is described as vindictive, we imply that it vindicates the force and majesty of the law. A law which anyone can violate with impunity has lost all force and authority. If the punishment appears as manifestly unjust and altogether disproportionate to the crime, then law is depreciated rather than enhanced by the infliction of the penalty. The majesty of the law must, however, be vindicated. Either a person should go entirely unpunished for every violation of law or else vindictive punishment is inherent in social organisation.

Punishment represents the denunciation by the community of the crime. In the case of Ananias and Sapphira, the wrath of God was manifested in vindictive action. Their action had struck against the very foundations of Christianity.

There is also a sense in which punishment needs to be preventive in character. The State has not only the right, but it has the duty to protect itself and its members from injury and loss. Preventive punishment removes from the offender the opportunity of transgressing in the same manner again. A driver of a car who has been repeatedly reckless may have his licence permanently cancelled. There is a necessity for removing the possibility of evil from those who are incapable of exercising certain functions belonging to citizens without abusing their privileges.

Just as punishment is said to be preventive when it aims to prevent the offender from repeating his offence, so it is said to be deterrent when it aims at deterring others from committing any similar crimes. "Exemplary" sentences, however, tend to treat the offender as an object-lesson rather than as a person. It is questionable whether it is right to regard an offender simply as an example through whom it can be demonstrated to other men that anti-social conduct does not pay.

While the reformation of the criminal is not the sole object of punishment it should always be one of the chief. Where reformation is impossible owing to the resistance offered by the individual the right to punish will of course remain. Those who enter the prison service are told that "the purposes of the training and treatment of convicted prisoners shall be to encourage and assist them to lead a good and useful life on discharge." It is further pointed out that "at all times the treatment of prisoners shall be such as to encourage their self-respect and a sense of personal responsibility. The aim is to get the offender on the side of the community and its laws."

In recent years there has been strong reaction against the use of corporal punishment both by the State and also by members of the teaching profession. One of the strongest arguments against its use relates to the brutalising effect it may have on those who have to administer it. It is extremely unlikely that in Britain and in the Western world generally we shall see a return to the use of corporal punishment. Punishment is more effective when it concentrates on public exposure and the resulting shame rather than on physical pain. Creative forms of punishment are to be preferred, like enforced work to repair damage done or to make reparation for loss. It is sometimes pointed out that men and women are sent to prison as a punishment and not *for* punishment. An emphasis on restitution and the personal relationship between the offender and the offended comes closer to a Biblical perspective (e.g. Exod. 21 18–19) than the impersonal idea of an offence against the State.

Explicit statements and implications found in both the Old and New Testaments would seem to give to the State the right of capital punishment in the case of murder, although a State may of course choose not to exercise that right. Our Lord in His parables accepted the right for the powers that be to take punitive measures against obstinate offenders and did not question the conclusion of His hearers—"He will put those wretches to a miserable death" (Matt. 21:41). Those who argue in favour of the retention of capital punishment usually quote the Mosaic "lex talionis" (Gen. 9:6), although they overlook the fact that in other respects the idea of "an eye for an eye and a tooth for a tooth" is not literally carried out. It should also be borne in mind that murder was not the only capital offence in the Mosaic code. Other examples were various sexual offences (Deut. 22, Lev. 20); kidnapping (Deut. 24:7); defiance of parental authority (Deut. 21:18, 21); blasphemy and incitement to apostasy (Lev. 24:16; Deut. 13). It is noteworthy that all these are outrages against the person, the family, the theocracy but *not* against property. Another point to be borne in mind is that under the Mosaic code punishment of death was not a cool, deliberate act on the part of society. The executioner was the nearest of kin to the one that was slain and was appropriately called "the avenger of blood". A number of arguments have been put forward against keeping capital punishment. The possibility of an innocent person being sentenced to death through human fallibility cannot be ruled out. It has been said that "Capital punishment belongs historically to a penal system based on violence of an unspeakably brutal kind; and the morality which allows this system to operate has for some years been in retreat before the advance of humanitarian and scientific influence." The question, however, arises whether life imprisonment is in fact a humane alternative to capital punishment.

It is often claimed that the retention of capital punishment for murder acts as a great deterrent. It can be argued, however, from statistics that capital punishment does not in fact deter. In 18th century England pickpockets were publicly hanged. At these executions other pickpockets took advantage of the large crowd to make a living! A further argument raised by those who favour abolition is along these lines—"How does the criminal pay for his crime by forfeiting his life? Victims cannot be brought back. Society is not enriched in any material way. And possibility of reformation on the part of the criminal is ruled out."

The question has to be faced, "Is capital punishment a divine imperative? Can we either from explicit statement or necessary inference prove from Scripture that governments are obligated by God to take the lives of certain types of killers?" We have already referred to the Apostle's manifesto on the punitive power of the

State (Rom. 13:4). The government is seen to be God's agent to perform acts of retributive justice. But it is debatable whether we may conclude from this that this mandate carries with it an express warrant for inflicting death. It is often claimed that Genesis 9:6 spells out a mandate for retributive killing. Are we justified, however, in extracting this one verse from its context and making it a universal law? In any case, is the demand for judicial retribution executed by secular impersonal governments the same as the demand for vengeance under Moses? We conclude that the Bible does not give us clear and sufficient evidence that God wills the State necessarily to take the life of murderers. It is questionable whether Christians are justified in insisting on capital punishment on the grounds that there is a divinely-given mandate for it in this day and age.

Before leaving the subject of crime and punishment we need to bear in mind that throughout the Bible runs the principle of equal justice for rich and poor together with the strongest denunciation of those who seek by bribery and other means to pervert justice. It can never be right if the rich may, at a price, buy the verdict they want, while the poor suffer. In our increasingly complicated and highly technical legal system care must be taken that all have equal opportunities for legal representation and that access to justice is truly equitable.

## 17. THE CHRISTIAN AND WAR

Consciences have not always been troubled by war as much as they are today. Indeed it is only in this century that the problem has become acute. Modern warfare and the horror of its effects have become grotesque.

In the Old Testament war was accepted as a normal part of the world order. Indeed, the Israelites established themselves by conquest and were sometimes called upon to wage war with the utmost ferocity (1 Sam. 15:3). Jehovah was sometimes referred to as the "Lord of Hosts", the "Lord mighty in battle" (Psalm 24:8). War was regarded as necessarily associated with the destiny of Israel (cf. Psa. 144:1). One must not give the impression, however, that the Old Testament picture of God is one of a deity delighting in war. He was a God of love and mercy. David was forbidden to build the Temple because of his having shed so much blood (1 Chron. 22:8).

The prophets foresaw a day when there would be universal peace (Isa. 9:2,4,7; 32:1,16,17). They spoke of the Messiah as "the Prince of Peace". Zechariah pictured Him as riding into Jerusalem on an errand of peace (Zech. 9:9).

In the New Testament there is no direct statement on the ethics of war as such, although there is unequivocal teaching about the need for non-resistance and lack of vindictiveness in personal relationships (Matt. 5:39, 43–44). Surprisingly perhaps there are also a number of military illustrations used (Matt. 8:9,10; Luke 14:31 ff.). On one occasion Jesus referred to an army as an instrument of judgment (Luke 19:41 ff.).

There is no suggestion that there is anything wrong in the soldier's calling as such. John the Baptist did not tell the soldiers who came to him to change their jobs (Luke 3:14). When Peter baptized the Roman centurion, Cornelius, he did not ask him to give up his profession. Our Lord Himself used a whip of cords to clear the Temple court, showing that He might be ready even to use violence in certain circumstances (John 2:15).

In the Olivet discourse our Lord spoke of future "wars and rumours of wars", (Mark 13:7), but He made it clear that as far as His Kingdom was concerned fighting had no place in it, (John 18:36).

Our Lord's words about buying a sword (Luke 22:36) have evoked considerable discussion—are they to be understood literally or figuratively? Most would favour a figurative interpretation. Christ is not telling His disciples either to repel force by force or to use force in the spreading of the gospel. He is saying in dramatic terms that they must be prepared to face a new situation, and in the struggle ahead must be just as determined and wholehearted as a soldier on active service, who gives up everything—even his cloak—so long as he only possesses a sword with which to continue the battle. The disciples, by taking our Lord literally, completely missed the point.

It was accepted in the Early Church that a Christian should not engage in warfare. The Early Christian Fathers united in condemning war as inconsistent with Christianity.

Tertullian held that the words "all they that take the sword shall perish with the sword" implied that a Christian should not serve in the army. He pointed out that all the conceptions and principles of Christianity were opposed to those of the Emperor. Origen in his letter to Celsus maintained that although Christians could not literally take up arms for the Emperor they nevertheless "fought" for him in offering their prayers for righteous government (1 Tim. 2:1–2). Another leader in the Early Church, Lactantius, stated: "It is not lawful for a just man to engage in warfare." Yet another Church leader, Basil, records that soldiers after being discharged from military service were excluded from Holy Communion for three years.

This attitude largely changed when Christianity became the established religion of the Empire in 312 A.D. From then onwards service in the army was regarded as meritorious, and the Cross actually became a military emblem. Pope Boniface VIII (1302) in his notorious Bull "Unam Sanctam" claimed that the Pontiff has the God-given right to wield two swords—the spiritual and the secular. Nevertheless there have always been minority groups who have taken a stand for pacifist principles. One thinks, for example, of the Waldenses, the Mennonites and the Society of Friends.

We shall look now at some of the arguments used by pacifists. The pacifist claims that in the New Testament there is an urgent call to compassion, to forgiveness and to love. Christ calls men to love their neighbours as themselves (Matt. 7:12). The Christian must be peace-loving. Such love, it is claimed, inevitably excludes the killing of one's fellow creatures whether it is a question of individual murder or the more general killing which war occasions.

Another argument used in favour of pacifism is that our Lord and His apostles always refused to fight. Our Lord's way of meeting evil and violence was the way of non-resistance, of turning the other cheek, and of returning good for evil (cf. Isa. 53). He consistently refused to meet the violence of His enemies, even with the supernatural powers that were available to Him (Matt. 26:53). Furthermore, our Lord stopped His disciples using violence against their enemies, and rebuked them for even wishing to do so (Luke 9:51–56; John 18:11). Even after Pentecost we find the apostles fleeing before threats of death (Acts 8:1,4; 9:25,30; 14:6; 17.10,14), and letting themselves be taken captive without offering resistance (Acts 4:3; 5:26, 41; 21: 30–33). There is only one reference in the New Testament to a disciple using arms, and he was rebuked for so doing (Matt. 26:51–52).

A further argument in favour of pacifism is that the New Testament never directly sanctions violence. Pacifists are quick to point out that Christians cannot model their ethical conduct solely on the Old Testament.

Some pacifists are ready to admit that a State under present conditions is bound in certain circumstances to wage war, either in order to protect its subjects or to fulfil treaty obligations solemnly undertaken, but they maintain that it is the duty of Christians to be pacifists in order to bear witness to the Christian ideal of "non-resistance".

Another argument put forward is along more pragmatic lines. Pacifists often contend that no good can ever come as a result of modern warfare, and that the outcome of a third world war would be disastrous to victors and vanquished alike. This argument has of course gained ground with the coming of nuclear weapons.

Whatever position we adopt, we must face the fact that as Christians we are "bound in the bundle of life" with the rest of the community, accepting its privileges and responsibilities. When this community is in extreme danger, as in time of war, has the Christian any right to say, "as a Christian I cannot share in the burdens of my fellow citizens for the sake of the community"? In actual fact, even the most ardent pacifist is bound to take some part indirectly in a modern "total" war, since as a tax-payer, however unwillingly, he is contributing towards the cost of nuclear missiles. Whereas the Christian must be non-violent in his private life, he is a member of a State which is committed to secure respect for order and justice. As such, it could well be argued, he must support the State to which he belongs, and, if need be, use violence in helping to defend it (Rom. 13:2).

It has generally been agreed that the only war in which a Christian may rightly take part is a "just war"—a war with a just cause and using just means—a war for defence rather than aggression. Some may well argue that the advent of nuclear weapons has removed the possibility of using "just means" in warfare, and also the likelihood of any balance of good resulting from a future war. Some Christians, therefore, feel they should refuse to take any part in a war in which their country uses nuclear weapons.

In the situation obtaining since the Second World War, we have had a "balance of terror", and nuclear weapons are referred to as the "great deterrent". As Professor D. M. MacKinnon has pointed out, given the emotional disturbance of a war situation, it is highly questionable whether escalation could be prevented—the use of tactical weapons could easily lead to a thermo-nuclear holocaust. The balance of terror is maintained by weapons which in the last resort men are prepared to use.

Both moral theology and international law recognise that there is a point at which warfare becomes barbarous and indefensible. Total war—warfare without any limitations as to the means and methods used—is in conflict with the Christian conscience and also with the conscience of the civilised world.

It has generally been held that area bombing is only justifiable when the area in question is directly related to the war effort. Modern nuclear weapons cannot be other than indiscriminate in their destructiveness. A war with nuclear weapons might possibly put an end to the human race, directly or indirectly. The use of such weapons becomes an act of wholesale slaughter with a measure of destruction altogether disproportionate to the end which the war was being undertaken to achieve.

In conclusion, we have to say that in neither the Old nor the New Testament is there any clear statement on the ethics of war as such, just as there is none regarding the ethics of slavery. The association of peace with righteousness and judgment is, however, a fundamental principle in Christian ethics. Obviously the Christian mind is in radical opposition to war as such as well as to those factors that lead to war. At the same time, the right of the State to use force, and even to take life in the maintenance of law and order, appears to be in accord with New Testament teaching. The conclusion reached by many Christians is that, although they must condemn war as evil, there are other dangers which are even greater. God's people should be concerned above all for righteousness, and this fact must also be taken into consideration. Peace bought at the expense of righteousness can hardly be the will of God. When justice is sacrificed to the desire for peace, violence has been done to the moral order of the universe. Occasions may arise when the State is morally bound to wage war. At such a time each individual Christian has to face up to his own personal duty in the matter. A man who, after deliberation, and with clear judgment, believes it is contrary to God's will for him to fight as a soldier must not do so whatever the consequences may be. On the other hand, the man who feels that as a citizen he is doing God's will by withstanding unrighteousness by force of arms, may be justified in his act—"let everyone be fully convinced in his own mind", (Rom. 14:5). Speaking about a Christian's position in a sinful society Professor Norman Anderson has said: "So often in human life, it is not a question of choosing between right and wrong. If it were so, it would be comparatively simple. So often we have to choose between two things, both of which are in some measure wrong." No one would question that war is in and of itself wrong, and results from human sin (James 4:1–2), yet in the society in which we live it could conceivably be the lesser of two evils.

## 18. RACE RELATIONS

The Old Testament recognises the fundamental unity of all mankind. Adam was made in the image of God (Gen. 1:27). Mankind is one by nature and experience. All men are a mixture of goodness and evil; all die; all are subject to moral and spiritual laws. As Creator, God is Father of all men, and recognises in all races and peoples those who seek Him (Acts 10:34, 35). The Bible presupposes only one standard of values. Men are valued in God's sight by their own inherent worth, and not by any outward differences. All people have a common origin and there is no basic difference in their biological make-up. (Acts 17:26). Furthermore, we recognise that there is a complete gulf between mankind and the rest of the animal world.

God's saving purposes encompass all men (1 Tim. 2:4). Man's basic need is the same whatever the colour of his skin, and God's provision to meet that need is in the one cross (Rom. 3:22,5:18; John 3:16). The physical appearance of man is an aspect of his life which concerns God least (Psa. 147:10). Different patterns of skin pigmentation have developed among men, but they do not necessarily provide a rationale for segregation. The Bible does not support a doctrine of inherent racial superiority.

When Israel was chosen by God to be "a special people unto Himself", this was not for her own sake but for the sake of all nations, that through her all the families of the earth should receive a blessing (Gen. 12:3). The prophet Amos made it clear that Israel's calling was not a capricious reward given to a favourite (Amos 3:2, 9:7). The 8th century B.C. prophets pointed out that since Israel as a nation had not been faithful in her high calling, God's promises and purposes would be fulfilled through a faithful remnant. The real calling of Israel was that she should be "a light to the Gentiles" (Isa. 42:6). It was never in the purpose of God that the people should develop a narrow and vindictive nationalistic spirit. In the book of Jonah we have a protest against such an outlook. Jonah was forced to realise the wideness of God's mercy shown in His compassion to the population of Nineveh, and even to the cattle there.

Our Lord, whilst recognizing the special relationship which Israel enjoyed (Matt. 10:6), nevertheless gave to His followers a world-wide commission (Matt. 28:19). In His personal dealings with men and women He showed a complete lack of racial prejudice (John 4:7; Luke 10:33). Pentecost was a further illustration of the world-wide scope of the gospel, although even some of the apostles were reluctant to shed their characteristic Jewish prejudices (Acts 10:14; 11:19).

The apostle Paul goes out of his way to emphasise that with the Christian Church racial barriers lose their significance (Gal. 3:28; Eph. 2:11–16; Col. 3:11). The issue was sorted out at the Jerusalem Council (Acts 15:12–29). The reconciliation of Jew and Gentile in the unity of the Church was a sign to the world of God's eternal purpose to sum up all things in Christ. If as Peter states, God is "no respecter of persons", He can even less be a respecter of colour. The non-elect is not the negro but the unbeliever, whatever his race or colour. The Christian Church does not ignore differences such as sex, social status and race, but in the power of the Spirit seeks to transcend them in a common relationship to the one Lord. Racialism may be defined as what happens when people recognise racial differences but do not accept the common humanity behind them. To quote the late Joost de Blank, former Archbishop of Capetown: "The new creation in Christ is the new patriotism which comes before any national or racial allegiance."

In spite of what appears to be the clear and consistent teaching of Scripture there are those who would claim a Biblical basis for regarding negro races as permanently inferior and subject peoples by divine decree. The argument is usually based on the curse put by Noah on the "sons of Ham" (Gen. 9:18–25) reducing them to slave status. It is assumed that the sons of Ham represent the black peoples. The argument is based on the flimsiest of foundations and a highly questionable interpretation of the passage. It is true of course that in Genesis, chapter 10, the descendants of Ham are said to include Cush, the Ethiopian, but they also include the Egyptians and the Canaanites who were of the same colour and stock as Israel. In any case, the curse which was made by Noah when in a state of intoxication was put on Canaan alone. The assumption that the curse rested upon the black races is made on the most unlikely identification of the Hebrew word "Ham" with the Egyptian word "Khem", meaning "dark". Where Ham is used in the Old Testament it is a name for the Egyptians and probably relates to the very dark *soil* of Egypt as compared with the much lighter Palestinian soil. It is significant that where Ethiopians are specifically mentioned in Scripture no derogative reference is made to the colour of their skin. In the book of Jeremiah we read of an Ethiopian who rescued the prophet and who was promised special deliverance (Jer. 38:6–13; 39. 15–18). The Ethiopian to whom Philip ministered (Acts 8:26–39) was addressed as on equal terms and the evangelist was happy to sit alongside him in his chariot.

The problem of race relations means different things at different periods of history and in different parts of the world. In the 1930's in Europe it took the form of anti-Semitism with the Nazi doctrine of the Herrenvolk, or master race. In the post-war years in Africa it has erupted in anti-white feeling on the part of the Mau mau in Kenya and later with the Simbas in what was then known as the Congo. In Nigeria it took the form of tribalism with bitter enmity between the northern Hausas and the eastern Ibos. Most of us today see it particularly in South Africa with its policy of apartheid, in the immigrant areas of Britain and in the clashes between negroes and whites in the United States of America. We shall concentrate our attention on the question of apartheid and on immigration.

In South Africa "apartheid" (separateness) is in fact, even if not in theory, indissolubly bound up with "baaskap" (white supremacy). The various Christian denominations in South Africa do not speak with one voice on the matter of apartheid. In the case of the Dutch Reformed Church segregation has been firmly entrenched for a very long time. It is commonly held that God deliberately diversified the human race, and that whilst the regenerate enjoy a mystical unity in Christ, on earth distinctions must be maintained. Segregation began as a practice and developed into a principle. While all races technically belong to the same Church they are expected to be attached to the separate churches within the Dutch Reformed Church which correspond to their particular racial grouping. Thus there is a church for whites, regarded as the mother church; a church for those of mixed race, and a church for the Bantu.

Most of the other denominations condemn in varying degrees the policy of apartheid, and it should be stated in all fairness that within the Dutch Reformed Church there are those who find themselves increasingly unhappy with government policy. At an earlier stage there were those, and there still are some, who genuinely felt that the black South African would ultimately benefit from apartheid. He would return to the natural setting of his homeland and he would avoid unpleasant racial tension. Some members of the Dutch Reformed Church stated quite clearly that they favoured "separateness" because they wanted to protect Africans from economic integration and therefore exploitation by unregenerate whites. Successive South African governments have assumed that whites in South Africa have a God-given right to self-preservation and to racial purity at any cost.

The more idealistic supporters of apartheid hold that the Bantu, or native South African, should be free to develop his own civilisation in his own way, and this is only possible when there is no interference by Europeans and no racial rivalry. William Lillie draws attention to certain fallacies in this reasoning—in point of fact "the European needs African labour in home and farm and mine, and the African is driven by economic need to seek a livelihood in European-controlled towns and industries." Furthermore, "the African has no desire to remain in the traditional civilisation of his past." Having seen Western ways of living, he realises that his village is commonly "a spot where sanitation is unknown, where disease stalks unhindered, where fear of witchcraft broods over all, where life comes down to the animal level".

No one would deny that the culture of the white South African is far superior to that of the Bantu, and he therefore tends to feel that it is his duty to see that his cultural heritage is not corrupted by close contact with Africans. Apartheid would appear to represent the fear of the white minority in the face of a black majority. In South Africa the kind of education that is provided for the Bantu is such as will fit him for the more menial tasks within the community, insuring that for at least the foreseeable future he will remain a "hewer of wood and drawer of water" for the ruling race.

The policy of apartheid, though technically calculated to maintain apartness, in fact imposes white racial supremacy on a dictatorial basis, and it has in fact helped to discredit Christianity in the eyes of the African. A World Council of Churches statement made in 1944 said, "Any form of segregation based on race, colour or ethnic origin is contrary to the Gospel, and is incompatible with the Christian doctrine of man, and with the nature of the Church of Christ". As William Lillie points out in *The Law of Christ*: "In Christ we do not value men for their race, but for what they are in themselves and in Him."

Before we consider some of the problems arising from immigration we will look briefly at the question of nationalism which is very much to the fore in the modern world. Nationalism has been defined as "the self-conscious assertion by a people of its own individuality in relation to other peoples". Nationalism starts with a love for a unit of territory, and in the case of formerly subjugated peoples this love is harnessed to a desire for political independence and self-expression. Toynbee has defined nationalism as "the worship of collective human power within local limits". The almost idolatrous devotion to the tribe or the nation seen in some areas of the world today is incompatible with true Christian internationalism. On the other hand, where nationalism is simply the self-conscious assertion of the people of their own corporateness it may be accepted as biblically sound (cf. Isa. 19:24–25). The Christian does not condone, much less approve, the view that powerful nations have the right to conquer and subjugate less powerful nations. While nationalism meets certain fundamental needs of man, because of its dynamic quality it may eventually manifest a tendency to pervert itself by giving itself up to the idolatrous worship of the State. Against any such tendency Christians must sternly set their faces. The

Christian Church must always be seen as a supranational organism. What is true of nationalism is, of course, equally applicable to tribalism.

Now for the vexed question of immigration. When two racial groups come into contact with one another one group has commonly lost its roots and is leading an unnatural kind of life. In addition there is often the difficulty of language. In such a situation friendly relations can easily become strained. Furthermore, there is usually a real difference in cultural outlook between such racial groups. There may be, and usually is, a great disparity in the standard of living also. One of the arguments used against allowing considerable numbers of immigrants to enter the United Kingdom is the danger of the British Isles becoming over-crowded. In this connection the number of those who migrate from this country must also be taken into calculation. There is also the danger of increasing unemployment. Here again, it should be borne in mind that many British industries at the present time depend largely upon immigrant labour, especially the woollen industry, the transport system and the medical services.

The problem of housing and the likelihood of intensifying slum conditions are frequently mentioned. The immigrant is often the victim of social inadequacies rather than the cause of them. Many immigrants are concentrated in certain areas because that is where they found work when they first came to this country. Because of colour prejudice many are forced to occupy old, often dilapidated, houses, and because of the pressure for accommodation many families share the same property.

It is sometimes argued that the presence of large numbers of immigrants leads to the lowering of educational standards in schools. Given equal opportunities, and a knowledge of English, the immigrant child usually holds his or her own with other children. There is no evidence that "whites" are basically superior in brain power to coloured people where they are nourished and educated under the same conditions. The alleged "slowness" of some immigrants is due not to inherent inferiority but to social conditions and a lack of knowledge of the English language. The real problem is that so many immigrants live, and their children go to school, in areas of deprivation.

When all is said and done migration is a feature of life in our world today, and without it further progress cannot be made. It is a phase of world development. It must not be seen simply as migration from the poorer countries to the wealthier, but a worldwide interchange of personnel and their skills. Obviously there must be some limits placed on the number of immigrants entering a given country in view of limited opportunities of work and of housing, but no Christian can be a party to stirring up strife against their immigrant neighbours.

Inevitably in a multi-racial society the subject of mixed marriages arises. The Ecumenical Synod of the Dutch Reformed Churches stated so long ago as 1958, "No direct scriptural evidence can be produced for or against the intermixture of races through marriage. The well-being of the Christian community and the pastoral care of the church necessitate, however, that due consideration be given to the legal, social and cultural factors which affect such marriages". Without losing our adherence to the principle of racial equality we need not necessarily encourage mixed marriages, though we permit them. There must be common ground in belief and outlook in those who are parties to a marriage. Biologically there is no reason why people of different racial origins should not marry and be happy together. Problems do arise, however, on account of the attitudes of society to the children of such marriages, although these attitudes may well change with the passing of time.

Let us sum up by saying that racialism implies denial of man's creation in the image of God, and is an affront to

God Himself. At the biological level there is no difference in the constitution of the blood groups which can be related to race or colour. Human blood has the same variations everywhere. Similarly, science has now proved that no conclusions about a person's intelligence or abilities can be drawn from his physical make-up. People differ according to their upbringing, their social background, education and innate capacity, but these differences run through the whole human family. It is naïve to speak of a pure race at this juncture in the world's history. From a biological point of view hybrid races are actually more vigorous than inbred ones. No modern nation-group is, scientifically viewed, a race.

The early Church stressed the unity of mankind, not only in creation, but in redemption. The happenings on the day of Pentecost gave dramatic evidence that it was God's will that His Church should be multi-racial. Soon the nerve centre of the Church changed from Jerusalem to Antioch, and from that cosmopolitan city the Church's influence radiated to every corner of the Roman Empire.

## 19. CHRISTIANITY AND CULTURE

Culture, according to one dictionary, is the training and refinement of manners and tastes. Modern anthropologists use the term to designate the distinctive way of life of a given society. Culture has been described as "the man-made part of the environment."

In looking at this subject Christians make two basic assumptions, namely, that God created the world and did so in an orderly manner, and that the whole of creation, including man, was affected by the Fall. When theologians speak of the total depravity of man they imply that man's whole nature was involved in the Fall, but that since man was created in the image of God, that image, though sadly blurred, remains.

The Christian recognises that God is the Author of all that is good and beautiful. Beauty is one significant aspect of God's glory. When the work of creation was complete, God pronounced it "very good" and whatever is "good" in God's sight must surely be beautiful. In spite of the Fall, as Calvin pointed out, God has left many gifts in the possession of mankind and if we despise such gifts we insult the Giver. Cultures vary enormously and Christians in common with the rest of the community have to relate to the particular culture of which they form part.

John Calvin insisted that those who studied in Geneva for the Christian ministry should have a wide cultural training such as he himself had enjoyed. The ever-recurring question is how far a Christian should become involved in purely cultural pursuits. Some people argue that cultural activities and interests are "worldly" and therefore beyond the pale for the Christian. The same people are usually the first to deplore inferior art and music and questionable television programmes! Dr. Frank E. Gaebelein, writing in *Christianity Today* a few years ago, took a rather different line when he complained of the "cultural illiteracy" of so many evangelical Christians. He wrote: "Art, which is the expression of truth through beauty, cannot be brushed aside as a luxury. We who know God through His Son who is altogether lovely must be concerned that the art we look at, listen to, read, and use in the worship of the living God has integrity!" In *The Christian and the Arts*, Derek Kidner points to one of the dangers of the complete rejection of all cultural pursuits—"For his neighbour's sake, if for no other reason, the Christian should beware of becoming a person of so few interests that he cannot even sustain a conversation, let alone a friendship, with anybody outside his religious circle. To have a *genuine* and discriminating pleasure in some human pursuit is to be halfway towards deserving human confidence; and without confidence people cannot be *led* towards the knowledge of Christ; they can only be prodded."

From the Scriptures themselves we can find little material on this subject. Man was given a mandate by the Creator which involved keeping the garden and having dominion over the earth. It was clearly the divine intention that man should subdue the earth and, as God's steward, develop its vast potential. At the same time the impression given in the Book of Ecclesiastes and borne out by experience is that "all is vanity" (cf. Rom. 8:20). When we come across seemingly contradictory viewpoints, it is often merely a case of differing emphases. Man is not intended to pursue culture merely for its own sake, but that is not to say that we are to renounce all interest in cultural pursuits.

Calvin ascribes to "the general grace of God" the fact that in His providence He has restrained the destructive forces of sin and preserved much that is culturally good in the world. We need to remind ourselves that the whole of creation is God's—"the earth is the Lord's and the fulness thereof" (Ps. 24). Paul in writing to Timothy speaks of "God who richly furnishes us with everything to enjoy" (1 Tim. 6:17), and he encouraged the Christians of Philippi to concentrate their thoughts on "whatever is true, whatever is honourable, whatever is just, whatever is pure, whatever is lovely, whatever is gracious". The same Apostle reminded the Corinthians that "all things" were theirs and in the list he gave he included "the world".

Granted that the world of culture has its legitimate place as far as the Christian is concerned; the question arises as to the place of moral judgment in relation to the arts. It would be fair to say that many art forms are too abstract to have more than the smallest common frontier with morality, although they may reflect in one way or another the moral climate in which they were produced, and reveal to some degree the basic philosophy of the artist. When the apostle Paul listed a wide range of interests upon which the minds of Christians might legitimately dwell, he ruled out, by implication, certain other interests which do not fall within those categories (Phil. 4:8). In another place he is more specific, stating that it is our Christian duty to "take no part in the unfruitful works of darkness, but instead expose them" (Eph. 5:11).

In the Bible itself we see life in the raw. There is no attempt to conceal some of the less pleasant aspects of human life, but where evil is exposed it is for a purpose not for its own sake. In evaluating a work of art, especially a piece of literature, the proper unit to consider is the whole work, not merely one particular part of it. In practice there is all the difference between focussing attention upon evil for its own sake, stimulating a morbid preoccupation with it, and giving a balanced picture of life as a whole. As Derek Kidner has pointed out: "There are Greek tragedies in which the chief components are hideous deeds and disasters, yet the dominant impression they leave is (within the limits of paganism) of the grandeur of the moral law".

From the aesthetic standpoint it is clear that differences of temperament, of race, and of generation will inevitably make for differences of appreciation. In the field of criticism the subjective and the objective are inextricably mixed. A distinction can, however, and must be made between what is basic and essential, and what is a matter of indifference. The fact that one man prefers the paintings of the Middle Ages to those of our own day is not, in itself, of any great significance. It is wrong to condemn something morally purely on the grounds that it does not appeal to us aesthetically. Obviously a Christian is bound to reject a work which is clearly calculated to deprave and which offends against public decency, although he must be aware that inevitably such judgments are subjective. In this whole area we need constantly to bear in mind that the artist or writer, and the critic and his judgment, are all affected to some degree by the Fall, and therefore any conclusions reached will be imperfect.

Before leaving this subject we should briefly refer to the relationship between our moral judgments and the differing cultures of the world. Modern missionary statesmen, such as Hendrik Kraemer, have tended to deplore the unconscious identification, on the part of earlier missionaries, of Christianity with Western culture. We must resist the temptation to think of any cultural expression as being the only Christian mode possible. We need to recognise relative values in different cultural patterns. The apostle Paul was able to distinguish between the unchanging supra-cultural message of the gospel and its adaptability to various cultures (1 Cor.

9:22). It is wrong, therefore, to take a Biblical injunction out of its cultural context and attempt to reproduce it without reflection upon its current significance. Our Lord enjoined His disciples to wash one another's feet, but few, if any, would think of literally fulfilling that command, at least in the West! Similarly, it could well be argued that whereas in the ancient world an unveiled woman would have been an object of shame, this is certainly not the case today in our Western civilisation. Obviously it is not always easy to decide whether a statement is normative for the whole Church in every generation or whether its application is specifically to the culture of the period when it was written. In his book, *Message and Mission*, Eugene Nida comments: "The selection of the Jewish people can be understood, in some measure, on the basis that God chose to reveal Himself through a people who, there at the crossroads of so many cultural influences at that point in world history, possessed a culture with greater similarities to a greater number of other cultures than has existed at any other time in the history of mankind."

## 20. PORNOGRAPHY AND OBSCENITY

It is difficult to arrive at a precise definition of pornography. In essence it implies the commercialisation and degradation of sex. In itself it is a symptom of an age of permissiveness and, many would feel, of a sick society.

In Great Britain a significant event was the publication in 1960 by Penguin Books of D. H. Lawrence's *Lady Chatterley's Lover*. The Director of Public Prosecutions was unsuccessful in securing a prosecution on the grounds that it was obscene and as a result there has been a flood of literature on the market which earlier generations would have considered quite unfit for publication. The basis on which Lawrence's book was cleared was that it did not contravene the Obscene Publications Act of 1959 which states that "an article is deemed to be obscene if its effect is, if taken as a whole, such as to tend to deprave and corrupt persons who are likely, having regard to all the relevant circumstances, to read, see or hear the matter contained or embodied in it." At the hearing it was agreed that the artistic and literary merits of *Lady Chatterley's Lover* were such that its publication was called for and that the sexual passages were more or less incidental.

Since 1960 there has been a spate of literature wallowing not only in eroticism, but also in sickening violence and brutality. Books which were once available only in "sleazy" bookshops in such areas as Soho in London are now freely available in general bookshops. In Sweden in February 1972 a Bill was passed by Parliament making it legal to publish, distribute and sell obscene pornographic literature. The only reservation to such sales required by this law is that sales posters on store fronts and other public places may not be "offensive". This new Swedish law, it would seem, has been so worded that the door is now open for public exhibitions of sexual perversities and even of violent scenes of a sadistic nature.

Mrs. Mary Whitehouse, whose campaign in Britain for public decency has been so derided by those who like to regard themselves as "pillars of the alternative establishment", has said this about pornography: "Porn, by its very nature, does violence to the true nature of sex and to the concept of love, respect and dignity of man without which civilisation as we know it will crumble. Implicit in the nature of porn, is an attack upon the concept of marriage, of family, of childhood and womanhood. The depersonalisation of sex, the exploitation of the human body, the appeal to sadism and the denigration of women, which are of the essence of porn, are all part of the attack upon the Christian ethic which has been the mainstream of democracy."

There can be no question about the change in attitudes discernible in recent years in the Western world in regard to what is permissible through the mass media. A growing number of publishers are producing pornographic books, many of which are distributed through mail-order businesses. Sex magazines, seeking to outdo one another in their erotic appeal, abound on street and station bookstands. In addition to these, there is the growing number of "underground" publications, most of which concentrate very largely on sexual material, much of which is grossly obscene.

From print we turn to the film industry where the same

trend is reflected. Nudity, once the preserve of the so-called "naturist" films, is now commonplace. Not content with the degree of licence granted to the ordinary cinema there have sprung up, in different parts of the country, cinema clubs where audiences are permitted to see films over which the authorities have no control whatever. Scenes of torture, brutality, sexual activity, bestiality and perversion are regularly shown on cinema screens up and down the country. Films purporting to convey sex education are circulating freely and most of them portray sex without any reference at all to moral values.

The theatre has, needless to say, followed the current trend with an ever increasing number of nude shows, and some recent plays on the London stage have been described by their backers as "elegant pornography". Strip clubs have mushroomed in recent years not only in Britain, but even more so in parts of Scandinavia. The general lowering of moral standards has been reflected in television programmes and as a result vigorous protests have been made by such people as Mrs. Whitehouse and her National Viewers' and Listeners' Association. The Festival of Light in the autumn of 1971 drew particular attention to pornography on the stage, in films and in books and magazines. The advertising world has, to some extent, jumped on the bandwagon by exploiting sex in order to sell a wide variety of goods which have no connection with the subject.

The real problem is to define what is obscene or pornographic. What is undeniable is that depersonalised sex is being exploited by the mass media for commercial gain and this in turn is bound to lead to a coarse, animalistic attitude to sexual relationships. The current tendency is to move away from "straight" sex to all kinds of deviations and perversions, and also to portray in the most vivid possible way sadism, violence and cruelty.

Those Christians who take a strong line regarding pornography are often accused of having "one-track minds" and it is suggested that they might be better employed attacking such social evils as homelessness, poverty, racial prejudice and violence. It is quite unfair to suggest that because someone is tackling a particular evil he is oblivious to other evils. The case against pornography is that a multi-million pound commercial transaction is being carried through by the blatant exploitation of something which is pure and good. Pornography exploits sex and in so doing devalues and depersonalises man.

In looking at this problem from a Christian point of view there are two main considerations. The first concerns the Christian attitude towards sex itself which has already been dealt with briefly in another chapter. The Bible glorifies marriage and sexual love, and nowhere is there any idea given that sex in and of itself is evil. The Bible, does, of course, tell us that man has fallen and as a result his whole nature has been adversely affected. Fallen man can very easily become obsessed with sex, and unscrupulous propagandists seeking commercial advantage are only too ready to suggest that sex is the only thing to live for. The Bible points out that sex is to be treated responsibly and that those who keep this instinct in its right perspective find more gratification and pleasure in it than those who deliberately inflame and excite it.

We are living in a materialistic age and when materialistic theories are applied to marriage and sexuality many strange ideas emerge. Love is said to be nothing more than sexual desire, and sex merely an expression of the flesh to be gratified as such. Those who hold to such a philosophy tend to revel in pornography and obscenity, since by such means their natural desires are stimulated. Commenting on the Longford Report (1972) a leader writer in the Daily Mirror said: "They have done a public service by exposing the extent of pornography in this country, and its unscrupulous exploitation for money...

they are right to pinpoint the grave social danger...a line HAS to be drawn somewhere about what is foisted on young people. Rape of young minds is as heinous as rape of young bodies."

The other consideration from a Christian point of view relates to the importance of the thought life. Christ Himself placed much stress on this (Matt. 15:19). He spoke of the lustful look as being tantamount to the deed (Matt. 5:28). Because we know our own hearts we realise the peril of "feeding the flesh". "Make no provision for the flesh", says the apostle Paul, "to gratify its desires". Books we may read, pictures we see, programmes we watch may so easily become a source of temptation to us, and the purveyor of pornographic literature is fully aware of that fact and literally trades on it.

This whole question of pornography raises inevitably the issue of censorship, the official scrutiny of material before it is published, exhibited or performed. Censorship is meant to provide a kind of sieve to prevent what is likely to deprave from ever reaching the public.

While it is the right and duty of public authorities in certain circumstances to safeguard the moral interests of the community it is often argued that censorship tends to be a mark of tyranny, whereas freedom of speech and expression is the mark of a mature community. Those opposed to censorship usually claim that some forms of pornography act less as a stimulus to action than as a safety valve, allowing socially unacceptable activities to be expressed in fantasy rather than reality. In practice censorship becomes increasingly difficult to apply. The position has now been established in law that a work should be considered as a whole and account taken of overall literary merit. On these grounds books such as D. H. Lawrence's *Lady Chatterley's Lover* have passed through the sieve. The general effect of this legislation has been to make it virtually impossible to substantiate in a court of law a charge of obscenity. A society with the maturity to discriminate could no doubt dispense with censorship, but it is highly questionable whether we have such a society and therefore it may be argued that men and women, and particularly the young, need to be protected by some form of censorship however distasteful that may seem to this age of permissiveness.

Writing in *Spectrum* in May 1971 David Holbrook comments, "Of course it's extremely difficult to decide (what is obscene) and many problems of freedom are involved but when it comes to indecent exposure or racial propaganda we must obviously maintain institutions in which people decide what is tolerable and what is not. Why should similar decisions not be taken about propaganda for perversion?"

Considerable interest in the subject of pornography was aroused by the publication of the 520-page Report of Lord Longford's Commission in the autumn of 1972. The Report produced a new definition of obscenity as covering "an article or performance of a play if its effect taken as a whole is to outrage contemporary standards of decency, or humanity accepted by the public at large." The Report made a number of recommendations although, of course, it had no official imprimatur. It was urged that penalties for convictions under the Obscene Penalties Act should be considerably increased, and that prosecutions should be brought against those who "for purposes of gain induce others to take part in any obscene or indecent performances to be shown in public or as models for any photographs or films of a similar kind." The Report urged that the cinema, sound and television broadcasting should be brought within the purview of the Obscene Publications Act. It was also urged that it should be illegal in future "to display in a street or other public place, any written or pictorial material which was held to be indecent." How far the recommendations of this Commission are likely to be taken seriously remains an open question, but there are indications that the general public is beginning to react against the spate of questionable publications which have appeared in recent years, and the police are also showing signs of taking a stronger line with those who disseminate pornographic material.

## 21. POLLUTION AND ECOLOGY

We are beginning to realise something of the heavy price which is being paid for progress. As someone has put it, "the affluent society has become an effluent society." One of the great problems of our time is pollution. We are facing the effects of our gross abuse of the natural environment: our air, water and land. As one speaker to American Congressmen stated, "We will go down in history as an elegant, technological society struck down by biological disintegration for lack of ecological understanding." The dimensions of the problem of pollution are quite frightening.

There is the fact of air pollution. A cartoon in the *New Yorker* pictured a wife sitting down to dinner on the terrace of a high-rise apartment and calling impatiently to her husband, "Hurry, dear, your soup is getting dirty." There are great industrial areas which at times are blanketted by smog, a word which incidentally has been coined in our post-war world. The result is that in some urban localities the incidence of respiratory ailments is excessively high. It would seem that the prophecy found in the Book of Revelation about the sun and the air being darkened by smoke is not so far removed from present reality (Rev. 9:2). Our factories are continually belching out toxic fumes into the atmosphere. As our roads become blocked with cars sending nitrogen oxide and carbon monoxide into the air so the problem increases. It is estimated that two thirds of the air pollution hanging over American cities is due to cars. It would seem that the invention of the internal combustion engine has proved a mixed blessing.

Attention has recently been focussed on the effects of certain pesticides and artificial fertilizers on our health. The spraying of such substances as D.D.T. has been called in question. Man is poisoning his environment. He introduces pesticides of ever-increasing potency, whose long-term effects on health have yet to be fully realised.

Water pollution poses yet another problem. The press is constantly focussing attention on instances of the widespread destruction of wildlife and of the fouling of our waterways. Every year countless millions of tons of chemical waste are poured into the sea and into our rivers.

The land is becoming despoiled by our failure to deal with the problem of disposing, much of our solid waste material. It has been computed that the average American produces more than five pounds of solid refuse per day, in human waste, glass bottles and tin cans, plastic bags and broken or worn-out utensils and playthings. What goes for an American applies to the rest of us in varying degrees. In his State of the Union Message in 1970, President Nixon said: "The great question of the 1970's is: Shall we surrender to our surroundings or shall we make peace with nature and begin to make reparations for the damage we have done to our air, to our land, and to our water?"

Modern man, quite rightly, is becoming increasingly concerned about environmental conditions and the word ecology has become familiar to most of us. There is, of course, nothing new about this. The American naturalist, George Perkins Marsh in his book *Man and Nature*, published in 1864, pointed out "the dangers of imprudence and the necessity of caution in all operations which, on a large scale, interfere with the spontaneous arrangements of the organic or inorganic world." The concern which Marsh expressed over a century ago is now being felt by men and women in general, so much so that we have had a National Conservation Year when attention was focussed on the problem.

The fact is that modern man with his highly sophisticated techniques has been guilty of disturbing the balance of nature—the ecosystem—to an alarming degree. As Dr. Stanley G. Browne writes in *Human Ecology—a Christian Concern*: "Whether we are dealing with carcinoma of the lung in Britain, or kwashiorkor in Nigeria or East Pakistan, or the overcrowded towns and villages of India, or the pollution of Lake Erie, there must be a recognition of an ultimate power to which, or to whom, individual human beings are in the end responsible and accountable." Browne goes on to state that "for some years now, Man has been playing at God, ecologically speaking, disturbing delicate balances of Nature with irresponsible cocksureness." As we look at the world scene today we find countless examples of exploitation—deforestation, over-cropping and over-grazing, soil erosion, the sterilizing of vegetation by chemical poisons—all for quick gains and with little or no thought for the future.

What has the Christian to say to all this? There is a body of opinion that believes, as Dr. Stanley Browne says, that "the basic cause of Western man's destructive attitude towards nature lies in Judeao-Christian traditions." Such an accusation is based largely on the assumption that man's increasing mastery over nature and the phenomenal explosion in scientific knowledge have received every encouragement from the so-called Christian nations of the world. Be that as it may, we ought to go back to first principles and discover afresh the truly scriptural standpoint.

In Genesis chapter 1 verse 28 man is told "Be fruitful

and multiply, and fill the earth and subdue it; and have dominion over the fish of the sea and over the birds of the air and over every living thing that moves upon the earth." In the following verses man is told how life on this earth is to be sustained and replenished. Men and beasts were to feed on the vegetation the Creator had provided. Following the Fall, man was faced with the fact that the task of "subduing" the earth was to be that much harder; there were now thorns and thistles to contend with.

After the flood, Noah was again commissioned "to be fruitful and multiply" and it seems that there was now a new food chain; man was given the other animals as well as vegetation for food (Genesis 9:1–7).

One could argue from such passages that the world of nature was clearly given to man for his exploitation. Yet there are in the Old Testament at the same time ethical and religious preconditions. Men are to love God and their neighbours. They are to act responsibly. The Biblical ethic calls for careful stewardship and cultivation of resources which after all are God's and not man's. No true Christian can act from motives of pure self-interest giving no thought to the long-term effects of his actions. The so-called Golden Rule provides an inviolate criterion for our uses of the resources of nature. To quote Dr. Browne again: "The resources of this world are not man's, but God's. The inexorable laws of nature cannot be flouted with impunity by anybody. The great issues of overpopulation, of world poverty, of pollution of the environment must be studied and solved in a Christian context. The Divine Intelligence that must be at the back of this most rational and complex of universes, requires the obedience and compassion of men and women who acknowledge their responsibilities to Him and to their fellows. 'The fear of the Lord is the beginning of wisdom'."

In facing these issues we need constantly to bear in mind that God created an orderly universe and therefore we should keep to a bare minimum the element of disorder. Deliberate unbalance and capricious destruction of natural resources are activities to be stoutly resisted. Man has a privileged position within the created order but privilege means responsibility. He is both a steward and a custodian of the natural order and it is not for him to squander the resources put at his disposal. We quote from an article in *The Christian Graduate* by Dr. John Paterson (March 1971). "The goal of normal conservation policy is not to use *no* resources—which is by definition impossible—but to achieve a 'steady state', in which the *rate* of use is adjusted to the combined rates of technological and natural replacement... This goal, with its assumption of a duty both to the present and to future generations of resource users, is in keeping with Christian thought. The Christian will be against wanton slaughter and conspicuous consumption but in favour of reasonable measures of management and in favour, too, of technical development, which is necessary not merely to support the larger population of the future but that of the present too, if living standards are to go on rising."

In an excellent booklet, *Ecology and Ethics*, Dr. R. J. Berry comments on the dominion which God gave to man (Gen. 1:28)—"This dominion is best understood as a mandate from God to work with the natural world in the role of a manager or steward, responsible as it were to a non-executive director... The Bible pictures man in his relation to nature as a shepherd, a farm manager, or a household steward. Consequently he has a real (as distinct from abstract) role in caring for the available resources on behalf of his boss—a role which allows him to make use of the resources for his own needs, but does not permit him to destroy them, since they are entrusted to him only for a limited period." It could perhaps be added that in some cases Christians have been so concerned to stress the fact that man stands apart from the rest of creation that they have failed to give sufficient place to man's responsibility in the stewardship of natural resources.

Undoubtedly we shall be hearing a great deal more in the years to come about ecology, pollution and conservation. It is encouraging that twentieth century Christians are recognising more and more that such topics are to be viewed against the background of Scripture. It is noteworthy that when the children of Israel were given a "land flowing with milk and honey" they were also given clear instructions as to the use they should make of that land (Leviticus 25). As Christians we do well to remember that God is both Creator and Redeemer and that, although ours is a fallen world, He is still interested in it.

## 22. A QUESTION OF CONSCIENCE

Many problems have been raised. All sorts of issues have to be resolved. It is not always possible to fit a precise text of Scripture to a particular issue and leave it at that. It is appropriate, therefore, that in the last chapter we should turn to the question of conscience, and touch on the art of casuistry.

Conscience has been defined as "the faculty or principle which pronounces upon the moral quality of one's actions or motives, approving the right and condemning the wrong" and "the ethical sense organ in man". Kant defined conscience as an instinct to pass judgement upon ourselves in accordance with moral laws. . .its judgment being not logical but judicial —"the categorical imperative". Aquinas defined conscience as "the mind of man making moral judgments". Here is yet another definition—"the testimony and judgment of the soul which gives approbation or disapprobation to the acts of the will". The Greek word translated "conscience" means literally "knowledge held in conjunction with another".

The New Testament particularly emphasises the painfulness of conscience in relation to the remembrance of past sins. Although there is no Old Testament word corresponding to "conscience", the fact of conscience is clearly recognised. Thus we read "David's heart smote him" (1 Sam. 24:5). In the Old Testament, the word "heart" is often the nearest equivalent to our English "conscience" (cf. Job 27:6; Psa. 32:1–5; 51:1–9). In the Old Testament "integrity of heart" is closely akin to what we mean today by a "clear conscience".

Conscience is innate in man (cf. Rom. 2:14–15). Conscience is not, however, the ultimate criterion. Conscience is not an intuitive "voice of God within us", but, rather, the faculty for hearing that voice. Conscience can be corrupted and misled. It is developed by the individual and the environment in which he lives. Thus all men possess a moral sense, but the standard of moral law varies.

The Christian recognises that he needs objective and reliable standards which he can fully and reasonably accept as his own, such as the Word of God and the example of Christ. It is by reference to these standards, and supremely through the work of the indwelling Holy Spirit, that a Christian man's conscience is enlightened.

The expression—"for conscience sake"—is found three times in the Authorised Version of the Bible, (Rom. 13:5; 1 Cor. 10:27; 1 Peter 2:19). In Romans 13:5 submission to the civil magistrate is enjoined, "not only to avoid God's wrath, but also for the sake of conscience". The "conscientious objector" faces not only any physical punishments that the State may impose, but also heart-searching and pain, because of the stand he feels compelled to take. In 1 Corinthians 10:27 the Corinthians are told not to ask questions as to the source of meat sold in the shops or provided at a non-Christian neighbour's table, "for conscience sake". Here again, the expression means "to avoid the pains of conscience". Conscience, here, is seen to be relative to knowledge, and it is when a man has learned that the meat has been offered to idols that conscience is roused. Furthermore, we learn that it is a definite Christian duty to avoid causing *other* people pains of conscience. In 1 Peter 2:19 the literal translation is, "If on account of conscience of God one endures pain, suffering unjustly". The unjustly persecuted man, like the man who resists the authority of the State, may sometimes be afflicted with painful doubts—"Could I be wrong after all?"

We see, therefore, that "for conscience sake" in the New Testament always implies that conscience is the voice of God demanding obedience. The apostle Paul, however, did not regard "conscientiousness", in the sense of deliberately cultivating the pains of conscience, as a virtue.

Dealing with the matter of eating sacrificial meats (1 Corinthians chapter 8) Paul refers three times to "weak consciences" and twice to "weak people". Paul's great concern is not merely that a man should be guided by his conscience, but that nothing should be done to aggravate the pains of conscience of the weaker brother. The apostle points out that through the knowledge of the more sophisticated Christian, who wittingly or unwittingly leads a weaker brother to do things that cause him pains of conscience, "this weak man is destroyed". In other words, the weak man is so misled that he becomes what we should call today a "disintegrated personality". When the voice of conscience is habitually ignored, man is left with a seared conscience (1 Tim. 4:2).

There are a number of references in the New Testament to a "good conscience" (1 Tim. 1:5; 19; Acts 23:1; 1 Peter 3:16,21; Heb. 13:18; 1 Tim. 3:9; 2 Tim. 1:3; Acts 24:16). A good or clear or pure conscience is the conscience of a man like the apostle Paul who could look back and claim that he had not done anything which had caused him pains of conscience. The New Testament values as highly as modern psychiatry a "clear conscience toward God and toward men" (Acts 24:16).

We shall turn now to what is termed casuistry. Casuistry not only seeks to convert a doubtful conscience into a certain one, to make clear whether an action is right or wrong in itself, it also deals with issues where the pros and cons have to be carefully weighed. Casuistry denotes the application of general principles of morality to particular cases of conduct and conscience. In common parlance the word has unfortunately come to be associated with the mishandling of principle in order to justify a position or line of conduct. Our Lord attacked those Pharisees who utilised their piety to increase their self-esteem, and by their casuistry falsified moral values (Matt. 23:5–7, 16–24). While it must be recognised that casuistry may be misused it is nevertheless indispensable in deciding the rights and wrongs of detailed issues in relation to basic Christian principles.

The New Testament does not present us with a Christian lawbook, covering every detail of life. There are, of course, general principles, but there are many issues which remain open questions. For example, the duty to speak the truth is fundamental, but ought a doctor to tell the full truth to a nervous patient to whom any shock might prove fatal? The command "You shall not kill" is clear enough, but what of the soldier in wartime? Is he wrong to take life? What of capital punishment? Such questions as these have to be investigated and decided through the science of casuistry. Many of the issues relating to matters of sex have to be decided in the same way. There are cases where doubt arises as to what is the right course of action, and where conscience seems to give no clear guidance—at such times we indulge in casuistry. Casuistry presupposes moral theology, and moral theology functions through casuistry.

Christians generally—with varying emphases—tend to decide ethical uncertainties by referring to various criteria, the most important of which is the Bible itself. The genuine seeker after truth wants to know what, if anything, the Bible says on the issue in question. He may then go on to enquire what is enjoined by Christian tradition. The next stage is to decide what may be logically inferred from Scripture and/or tradition.

Moral theologians have deduced different ways of attempting to settle the right course of action when in doubt. The rigorist argues that if there is any doubt about a certain course of action, then such action should not be taken. Taken too far this system may lead to over-scrupulousness. The rigorist argues that in matters of conscience the course of greater moral safety should always be chosen. Another method involves weighing up the pros and cons and choosing that course of action which seems to be supported by the most weighty arguments. The weakness here is that doubt often exists as to the relative merits of the pros and cons. When the pros and cons seem evenly balanced then liberty must be granted. It is also argued that due consideration must be given to the gravity of the case under review and possible effects following the particular decision made. The more serious the issue the more we must tend to strictness.

Principles which Paul laid down in relation to the issue of eating or not eating meat sacrificed to idols have often been cited as providing useful guide-lines for Christian conduct in other directions. In matters such as this his advice was "Let everyone be fully convinced in his own mind" (Rom. 14:5). Furthermore, he added "Let us no more pass judgment on one another" (Rom. 14:13). Incidentally, it is somewhat ironic that people who pride themselves on their tolerance are often very intolerant of those stricter than themselves! There was a third criterion which the apostle set forth—"Rather decide never to put a stumbling-block or hindrance in the way of a brother" (Rom. 14:13, 21; cf. Matt. 18:6). A stronger brother may in matters indifferent accommodate himself to the scruples of a weaker brother (1 Cor. 8; Gal. 2:3–5).

If in Christian ethics we are looking for the provision of a detailed legal code we shall be disappointed. From the New Testament no such legal code is forthcoming. Instead, it speaks of the divine initiative taken in man's salvation and proclaims God's redemptive acts in and through the Death and Resurrection of our Lord Jesus Christ. It puts to us the question: "What sort of men ought those to be who have experienced God's grace in Christ?" Although it gives no direct or detailed answer to many of the social and political problems of our time, it impels us to judge these in the light of what we know our God to be through the revelation of Himself in Christ. Because we live in a community made up of sinful men and women and because we ourselves are affected by the Fall, we shall find that at times our judgments are coloured by wrong motives. We shall also frequently be called upon to face issues in which the only course of action open to us is to decide for the lesser of two evils. It would be entirely wrong, however, to suggest that we have been left in the dark as far as God's basic requirements are concerned. Our need is to pray for grace and strength to take the path we come to know as the right one.

## EPILOGUE

The phrase "social gospel" was very much in vogue during the first half of the present century. No doubt it meant different things to different people, but the general impression it conveyed was that the Christian message was essentially related to the amelioration of life here on earth, and offered a kind of blue print for a just society. Preachers spoke of "bringing in the Kingdom" and, for some of them at least, this meant little more than improving the lot of the less privileged members of the community.

Before World War I and to some extent after it, there was abroad a Utopian idealism which genuinely believed in man's perfectibility and inevitable progress. This naïve optimism about human nature has since been utterly discredited by facts. In those days it was thought that improved education coupled with the onward march of science and technology would pave the way for a brave new world. During the tragic years of World War II my former Principal, Dr. John S. Whale, lecturing on Christian Doctrine in Cambridge, said: "Our generation is rediscovering the abysmal depths of evil in the heart of man, and realising that Public Enemy Number One is neither ignorance, nor stupidity, nor the defective social environment, but *sin*, which is the deep mysterious root of all these evils." He was right, and today most thoughtful people would not need very much convincing of that fact. The concept that the human race is steadily moving forward in the direction of Utopia is certainly not a Biblical one. The parable of the Wheat and Tares bears witness to a very different climax to human history. Commenting on that parable, Archbishop Trench wrote: "Evil is not as so many dream, gradually to wane and disappear before good; but is ever to develop itself more fully. Even as on the other side good is to unfold itself more and more, and more mightily also. Thus it will go on until at last they stand face to face, each in its highest manifestation in the persons of Christ and of Antichrist. Both are to grow, evil and good, till they come to a head, till they are ripe, one for destruction and the other for full salvation."

We state this lest anyone should fondly imagine that we seem to hope for an eventual Christian society on earth. We are under no such illusion. On the other hand, is the alternative to such illusion to stand by and do nothing? Should we concentrate on proclaiming personal salvation with its promise of life beyond the grave and do nothing to alleviate human suffering here and now? Our Lord's teaching when He spoke of the sheep and the goats would suggest otherwise. We are to be concerned for men's physical and material wellbeing here and now as well as with their eternal destiny. It is not a case of "either or" but of "both and". As we have already pointed out, this is no new note for evangelicals to strike. Kathleen Heasman in her appraisal of social work carried out by evangelical Christians in the 19th century, *Evangelicals in Action*, points out that whilst theirs was essentially a personal religion which regarded salvation as more important than life on earth, they nevertheless were acutely aware of the appalling social conditions of the time and were extremely active in their efforts to bring about a healthier state of affairs.

Today we have a Welfare State in Britain and it might be thought that most, if not all, social and material problems are taken care of by the authorities so that Christians are free to concentrate solely on spiritual matters. The situation is far different. Our complex society has spawned a whole new set of problems which demand our urgent attention—problems that largely spring from such areas as automation, advanced medical and surgical techniques, increased mechanisation, longer leisure hours, and a greater degree of affluence than any previous generation has known.

Some might be tempted to think that because our world is so vastly different from that of New Testament times the Bible has no relevance to our modern technological society. This is very far from the truth. Obviously we do not look in the New Testament for cut and dried answers to every question which arises in our minds, but it was never more necessary to "search the Scriptures" and discover those Biblical principles which impinge on every aspect of human life. The sheet anchor in all our thinking is the Biblical estimate of man himself, made in the image of God. Every conclusion we reach must be related to the Christian doctrine of the dignity of human personality. While it is only too obvious that man is a fallen creature and that, as John Whale pointed out, "under sufficient stress the modern man, not to mention the modern woman, will do deeds of evil as terrible as anything recorded in history", the fact remains that he is still God's creation, made in the divine image and endowed with gifts that set him above all other creatures. It is precisely because God is who He is, and man is who he is that Christian ethics is so important. In saying this we are bound to remind ourselves that Christian ethics are the ethics of the Kingdom of God and for that reason there will always be a gap between what God demands and what fallen man achieves or even sets out to achieve. The fact remains, however, that

Christians are called upon to be both the salt of the earth and the light of the world and they should be concerned to do all in their power to bring Christian influence to bear on society—"Live as free men, yet without using your freedom as a pretext for evil; but live as servants of God. Honour all men. Love the brotherhood. Fear God. Honour the emperor." (1 Peter 2:16–17)

# SOME SUGGESTIONS FOR FURTHER READING


*General*

| | |
|---|---|
| Anderson, J. N. D. | *Into the World*—Falcon Books. |
| | *Morality, Law and Grace*—Tyndale Press. |
| Barclay, William | *Ethics in a Permissive Society*—Fontana Books. |
| Barry, F. R. | *Christian Ethics and Secular Society*—Hodder and Stoughton. |
| Cave, Sydney | *The Christian Way*—Nisbet. |
| Hastings, A. W. & E. | *Important Moral Issues*—T. & T. Clark. |
| Hoffman, George | *Let's Be Positive*—Scripture Union. |
| Lillie, W. | *Studies in New Testament Ethics*—Oliver and Boyd. |
| Lillie, W. | *The Law of Christ*—The St. Andrew Press. |
| Marshall, L. H. | *The Challenge of New Testament Ethics*—Macmillan & Co. Ltd. |
| Triton, A. N. | *Whose World?*—Inter-Varsity Press. |
| Wood, Thomas | *Some Moral Problems*—S.C.M. |

*Sermon on the Mount*

| | |
|---|---|
| Lloyd Jones, D. M. | *Studies in the Sermon on the Mount (Vols. I and II)*—Inter-Varsity Press. |

*Sex Ethics*

| | |
|---|---|
| Derham, A. M. | *Love, Sex and Marriage*—Hodder and Stoughton. |
| Gardner, R. F. R. | *Abortion*—The Paternoster Press. |

Scorer, C. G. — *The Bible and Sex Ethics*—Tyndale Press.
Thielicke, H. — *The Ethics of Sex*—James Clarke and Co. Ltd.

*Industry*

Catherwood, H. F. R. — *The Christian in Industrial Society*— Tyndale Press.
Deeks, Frank — *Shop-Floor Christianity*—Inter-Varsity Press.

*Citizenship*

Catherwood, H. F. R. — *The Christian Citizen*—Hodder and Stoughton.
Griffiths, Brian (Ed.) — *Is Revolution Change?*—Inter-Varsity Press.

*Race Relations*

Bronnert, David — *Race*—C.P.A.S.
Edgington, David — *Christians and Colour in Britain*—Scripture Union.
Gladwell, Joyce — *Brown Face, Big Master*—Inter-Varsity Press.
Hill, Clifford — *Immigration and Integration*—Pergamon.
Wood, Downing — *Vicious Circle*—S.P.C.K.

*Pollution and Ecology*

Browne, J. F. — *Human Ecology—A Christian Concern*—Christian Medical Fellowship.
Berry, R. J. — *Ecology and Ethics*—Inter-Varsity Press.
Kidner, D. — *The Christian and the Arts*—Inter-Varsity Press.

*Pornography and Obscenity*

Russell, Norman — *Censorship*—Inter-Varsity Press.

*also published by*
*Scripture Union*

## UNDERSTANDING THE BIBLE

by John R. W. Stott

Is the Bible still meaningful? Why, in fact, was it written? Can it be trusted? What, really, is its message? How is the Bible to be interpreted? How can we best use it today?

This book not only considers these practical questions, but also includes a valuably informative chapter on the lands of the Bible—and a bird's eye view of its contents that will give many Bible readers a new perspective. The Rev. John R. W. Stott is Rector of All Souls, Langham Place, in the heart of London. He is widely known as a preacher in Britain, America and other countries. His many previous books include *Basic Christianity*, which has been translated into several other languages. He is currently President of the Scripture Union Movement, which for nearly a hundred years has been helping people around the world to read and understand the Bible.